THE COMPARATIVE METHOD
IN
HISTORICAL LINGUISTICS

INSTITUTTET
FOR SAMMENLIGNENDE KULTURFORSKNING

THE
COMPARATIVE METHOD
IN
HISTORICAL LINGUISTICS

BY

ANTOINE MEILLET

Translated from the French
by
GORDON B. FORD, JR.
Assistant Professor of Linguistics
Northwestern University
Evanston, Illinois

PARIS
LIBRAIRIE HONORÉ CHAMPION, ÉDITEUR
7, Quai Malaquais

1967

This English translation of
La méthode comparative en linguistique historique
is dedicated to
Professor Calvert Watkins

TABLE OF CONTENTS

PREFACE

When Alf Sommerfelt informed me that the great institute newly created in Kristiania (now Oslo) on the initiative of Professor Fr. Stang, *Instituttet for Sammenlignende Kulturforskning* (Institute for the Comparative Study of Civilizations), intended to invite me to take part in the series of lectures which were to mark its inauguration, I immediately accepted with joy.

The young scholar who informed me of the invitation had worked for several years — years of the great war — among French linguists. To all the members of our small group he had become a friend. I was happy to meet him again in his own country, where linguistics owes so much to him, and to be able to work for a while with him again.

I was pleased to be associated with the beginnings of an institute from which the sciences of man are promised great results. We have hitherto done much with the facts at our disposal ; but the materials which are at the disposal of researchers have been often exhausted. The time has come to undertake large systematic investigations which will furnish new material and will enable us to enlarge and deepen the theories now accepted. Then again it is important to place in contact all scholars who are concerned with man and with his civilizations in all aspects : a language cannot be understood if we do not have an idea of the conditions under which the people who use it live ; and we cannot truly comprehend at all a religion or social customs without knowing the language of the people who practice these customs. The unity of the new Institute expresses the unity of the object which it studies—man. It is to be desired that similar organizations may be founded elsewhere and provided with large resources necessary for research.

Moreover, the subject which, in accordance with the organizers, I have chosen for these lectures is one on which the time has come to reflect. After some thirty years, during which we drew from the principles posed between 1875 and 1880 the results which could have been expected from them, historical linguistics has returned to a period of fermentation. New procedures of investigation have brought unexpected results. Never before have we made such an effort to reduce linguistic changes to « laws », even to « general laws », and never before have we tried so hard to grasp the most specific facts or to penetrate the very soul of the people among whom innovations are made. From the oldest languages where changes appear to us as reduced to mere schemes, to modern dialects where the facts are so concrete and

so particular that the details conceal from us the
main trends, we have observed infinitely varied facts.
Linguistics has come in contact with all the related
disciplines where we can hope to find explanations.
Though too slowly, the historical study of other
than Indo-European languages is progressing ; but
the procedures which have been successful in the
Indo-European domain are not equally utilizable
everywhere. We must reflect on the methods employed,
examine their legitimacy, and see how we might
extend their use and make them flexible — without
diminishing their rigor — in order to make them
conform to the requirements of research in new
domains.

It is all the more advisable to examine the methods
since in recent times many linguists have advanced
inadequately proven hypotheses. New etymologies are
found in profusion, and the majority are presented
in such a manner that we cannot perceive even the
beginning of a proof. It would be vain to criticize
them in detail as long as we are not in agreement
concerning the conditions which together demonstrate
the correctness of an etymological comparison. For
those who will admit that the principles presented
here are well founded, a large part of the complicated hypotheses which have been made about Proto-
Indo-European or some Indo-European etymologies
recently advanced will appear as hardly calling for
an examination. Although discussion has almost no
place in these lectures, one will find here implicit

criticism of many new works which do not satisfy the requirements of a rigorous method.

We have not proposed to present new ideas here, but only to determine in a precise way the circumstances in which the comparative method can and must be employed in historical linguistics. We shall be satisfied if the reader finds exactly indicated here the strength, but also the limits of this method.

The ideas developed here have been put in writing only after having been presented orally. Edited after having been delivered, these lectures take account of observations which have been presented to the author, in particular by Alf Sommerfelt whom I am happy to thank.

I wish — but it would be fanciful to hope — that these lectures may meet with a reception among the general public as indulgent and as kind as that which they received in Kristiania.

Kristiania (Oslo), September 1924.

A. M.

I.

DEFINITION OF THE COMPARATIVE METHOD

There are two different ways of practicing comparison : one can compare in order to draw from comparison either universal laws or historical information. These two types of comparison, equally legitimate, differ absolutely.

Beast fables are found everywhere in the world : the similarities between the different animals and man are such that it is natural to attribute to animals adventures comparable to those which happen to men and to express by them things which it would not be so easy to say directly. One can compare these stories with each other in order to define their forms, their characteristics, their use, and thus to make a general theory of animal stories. The agreements which are established result from the general unity of the human mind, and the differences from the variety of types and degrees of civilization. One thus succeeds in learning about the general characteristics of humanity, but does not learn anything about its history.

If one examines, as a young French scholar, Dumézil, has done, the Indo-European myths pertain-

ing to the drink of immortality, one obtains completely different results. The idea that there was a drink
capable of conferring immortality is too natural to
be characteristic. But when one finds in a more or
less complete way among the various Indo-European
peoples the legend of a beverage of immortality made
in a gigantic vat, and when to this legend is joined
the story of an untrue fiancée and the account of
a struggle between gods and demoniacal beings, there
is therein a set of singular facts which do not in
themselves have any connection with each other
and whose convergence cannot consequently be
fortuitous.

If the meaning to be expressed by language were
linked by a natural connection, loose or strict, to
the sounds which indicate it, that is, if by its own
value, apart from tradition, the linguistic sign evoked
an idea in any way, the only type of comparison
utilizable by the linguist would be the general type,
and all linguistic history would be impossible.

But, in fact, the linguistic sign is arbitrary : it
has value only by virtue of a tradition. If unity is
expressed in French by *un, une,* duality by *deux,* etc.,
this is not because the words *un, une — deux —,* etc.,
have by themselves any connection with unity, duality,
etc., but solely because such is the usage taught by
those who speak to those who are learning to speak.

Only the totally arbitrary character of the sign
makes possible the historical and comparative method
which will be studied here.

Take the numerals in French, Italian, and Spanish. We have a series :

FRENCH	ITALIAN	SPANISH
1. *un, une*	*uno, una*	*uno, una*
2. *deux*	*due*	*dos*
3. *trois*	*tre*	*tres*
4. *quatre*	*quattro*	*cuatro*
5. *cinq*	*cinque*	*cinco*
6. *six*	*sei*	*seis*
7. *sept*	*sette*	*siete*
8. *huit*	*otto*	*ocho*
9. *neuf*	*nuove*	*nueve*
10. *dix*	*dieci*	*dies*
20. *vingt*	*venti*	*veinte*
30. *trente*	*trenta*	*treinta*
40. *quarante*	*quaranta*	*cuarenta*
100. *cent*	*cento*	*ciento*

Such correspondences cannot be accidental ; they are all the less so as the differences between one language and another can be reduced to definite rules of correspondence. Thus the difference between *huit*, *otto*, and *ocho* is great at first sight ; but the fact that it is not accidental results from the situation that there is a series of similar correspondences, as Fr. *nuit*, It. *notte*, Sp. *noche*, or Fr. *cuit*, It. *cotto* ; and we have also Fr. *lait*, It. *latte*, Sp. *leche* ; Fr. *fait*, It. *fatto*, Sp. *hecho* ; etc. The agreements evident from the outset show the way to proceed. But the rules of phonological correspondences alone permit us to make use of them.

Where apparent similarities have indicated the right path, it often happens that some *singular* detail brings confirmation. It is significant, for example, that there is a distinction between the masculine and feminine for *un*, *une* and not for the other numerals.

We are thus led to posit that the numerals of French, Italian, and Spanish go back to the same original tradition. In such a case, experience shows that there are two possible types of tradition : the three groups considered can go back to a common origin, or else two of the three can have borrowed their forms from the third. In the case in question, the second hypothesis is excluded because one cannot explain the forms of any one of the three languages by those of another. Fr. *huit* cannot be derived from It. *otto* or from Sp. *ocho*, nor It. *otto* from Fr. *huit* or from Sp. *ocho*, nor Sp. *ocho* from Fr. *huit* or from It. *otto*. It is thus proved that the numerals of French, Italian, and Spanish have a common point of departure which is neither French nor Italian nor Spanish.

In the example chosen, the agreements are so numerous, so complete, and the rules of correspondences so easy to recognize, that they strike the layman immediately, and it is not necessary to be a linguist to perceive their convincing value. The agreements are less striking and the rules of correspondences more difficult to determine if we observe languages separated by larger intervals of space and time, like Sanskrit, ancient Attic Greek, Latin, and classical Armenian :

	SKR.	ATT. GR.
« one »	ékaḥ, ékā, ékam	hēs, mia, hen
	LAT.	ARM.
	ūnus, ūna, ūnum	mi

(where there are three forms, the first is masculine, the second feminine, the third neuter : Armenian does not have differences of grammatical gender.)

	SKR.	GR.	LAT.	ARM.
« two »	d(u)vā	duo	duo	erku

(we note here only the masculine forms where the gender is distinguished ; likewise for « three » and « four ».)

	SKR.	GR.	LAT.	ARM.
« three »	tráyaḥ	trēs	trēs	erekʿ
« four »	catvāraḥ	téttares	quattuor	čʿorkʿ
« five »	páñca	pénte	quinque	hing
« six »	ṣáṭ	heks	sex	vecʿ
« seven »	saptá	heptá	septem	ewtʿn
« eight »	áṣṭā [1]	óktō	octō	utʿn
« nine »	náva	ennéa	nouem	inn
« ten »	dáśa	déka	decem	tasn

1. Vedic form before a consonant, alternating with áṣṭāv before a vowel.

If, reservation being made for the numeral « one », the correspondences between Greek, Latin, and even Sanskrit are evident to a great degree, this does not hold for those between Armenian and the other languages.

But it is sufficient to examine the Armenian facts closely for the convincing value of the agreements to become evident.

Thus Arm. *erku* « two » does not resemble Lat. *duo*, etc. ; but other correspondences show that *erk-* can correspond to **dw-* of the other languages ; thus, just as Greek has a root *dwi-* for the idea of « to fear », Armenian has *erki-* (*erkiwl* « fear »), and just as Greek has an old adjective *dwārón* for « long », Armenian has *erkar* « long » (cf. below, p. 46). The agreement can thus be reduced to a general rule of correspondence : an old *dw-* becomes Arm. *erk-*.

For the first member of compounds, Greek has *dwi-*, and Armenian *erki-*. Thus there is a group of singular agreements which leave no doubt (see below, p. 128).

The Armenian forms *erek῾* and *č῾ork῾* are far from Gr. *trēs*, *téttares* ; but they can, at least in part, be explained by similar correspondences. And, characteristically, in Sanskrit as in Greek, « three » and « four » have case forms of an ordinary type, while the nouns from « five » on are invariable ; in Armenian, « three » and « four » have normal case forms and, in particular, the final *-k῾* is the mark of the Armenian nominative plural, a mark which is not found in the other cases.

Less apparent at first glance than the agreements among French, Italian, and Spanish, the agreements of the forms of the numerals in Sanskrit, Greek, Latin, and Armenian are fundamentally no less certain.

These agreements, which cannot be explained by borrowings from one language to another, presuppose a common origin. But it remains to interpret them in a systematic way : such is the object of comparative historical linguistics.

The process whose principle we have just seen may seem complicated and difficult to handle. But there is no other to do linguistic history.

For linguistic history is never done by means of a series of texts arranged in chronological order. If the linguist makes use of old texts, it is only to observe linguistic stages in them. It goes without saying that for all the ancient languages, the facts can be observed only with the aid of texts. It is from written documents that Attic, Gothic, classical Armenian, and Old Church Slavonic are observed. Interpreted critically, these documents furnish much, and we can often have an exact idea of certain ancient linguistic stages. But this study permits us to determine the state of a language only at a certain moment under certain conditions. The examination of texts is only a substitute for direct observation which has become impossible.

Even in the best cases, the written language is very far from registering exactly the successive changes of the spoken language. Often the written language is fixed, and the form which it presents hardly changes

from one century to another. Even when it is not
entirely fixed, written usage is ordinarily dominated
to a large degree by earlier forms — which are not
always known.

Take the classical example of Latin. Between the
written language such as is found in Plautus and that
which is found in St. Augustine, there are differences
of detail ; but the orthography hardly varies ; the
grammatical forms and the major part of the vocabulary remain the same. Philologists have taken great
pains to find differences between the periods of Latin
at different historical dates. They have brought to
this research all the minute precision which a
grammarian can provide. And they have in fact
established some slight differences ; but these differences are largely attributable to the literary genre :
the comedy of Plautus, designed for the general public,
is not comparable to the orations of Cicero or to
the bulletins of the purist Caesar. The language of
Hellenistic poetry is not that of Hellenistic prose.
There are also differences between one writer and
another. But, basically, only one Latin has ever been
written and taught in school.

Moreover, among the forms which the written texts
furnish, only comparison indicates those which have
a value for the subsequent history of the language.
To designate the ear, we find in Latin written texts
auris and also the derivative *auricula*. Nothing in the
old Latin texts indicates that one or the other of these
forms should prevail over the other ; *auris* is the

general form. But it is from *auricula* that the forms
of the Romance languages are derived : Fr. *oreille*,
It. *orecchia*, Sp. *oreja*. Only comparison of French,
Italian, Spanish, etc. gives information about the
form which serves as a basis for the Romance
languages.

On the other hand, the language which has survived
is not that which was written. Between literary
Latin, which is preserved by the texts of the authors,
and spoken Latin, which the Romance languages
continue, there were differences varying with individuals and their degree of culture. The Romance languages do not continue literary Latin. The word for
« mouth » in written Latin was *os* ; but what has
survived is the popular noun *bucca*. And so in a lot
of cases.

Even when texts of different periods furnish
successive linguistic stages, we do not observe a continuity. The essential changes to which is due the
passage of the old Latin type to the Romance type
took place between written Latin and the first monuments of the Romance languages. Without doubt the
people who wrote Latin from the third to the tenth
century A.D. let many forms slip out which were
not correct in earlier Latin and which were due to
the already completely different language which they
spoke ; but one can only appreciate the value of these
lapses and recognize therein linguistic evidence as a
result of a knowledge of the Romance languages. In
the Latin texts written from the imperial period to

the Carolingian period by people uneducated enough
to let slip mistakes against classical usage there is
some information, especially in the chronology of
events, for the comparative grammar of the Romance
languages. But if the light which these texts cast is
precious, it is to clarify comparison ; if the comparison happened to be lacking, the light would be
lost in the void. If the Romance languages had died
before being written down, we would perceive that
classical Latin was corrupted ; but we could not form
any precise and complete theory of the changes
which had taken place. The essence of linguistic
change takes place outside our view.

The history of Persian furnishes a still more noteworthy example. We know — in a very incomplete
way, it is true — Persian at the time of Darius and
of Xerxes, thanks to the monumental inscriptions of
these kings. Afterward, evidence is lacking from the
fifth century B.C. to the the third century A.D. Then
we find Pahlavi.

But, in the first place, this Pahlavi is not, as was
believed until recent years, the continuation of the
dialect in which the inscriptions of the Achaemenid
sovereigns were written : just as I have myself indicated and as Tedesco has demonstrated in a more
precise and more complete way, the Pahlavi of the
texts of the Sassanid period, the ancestor of literary
Persian, presents some features which distinguish it
from Achaemenid Persian. Thus we cannot say
that the linguist possesses here the tradition of the

same language ; he observes at different dates two dialects of very close, but not identical type.

In the second place, between Achaemenid Persian and Sassanid Pahlavi, there is a difference of development as great as that which separates old Latin from Romance. Between the two dates the language has changed its character. As in the Latin domain, the essential part of the change has taken place outside the view of the historian. The linguist has available two linguistic stages profoundly distinct from each other ; to write a history, it is necessary for him to reconstruct the intermediate stage. Comparison of the various modern Iranian dialects aids in making this reconstruction ; but it furnishes only directions, not positive evidence.

Generally, linguistic history is thus done only by comparing linguistic stages with each other. For the facts furnished by a succession of texts, in the exceptional cases where those who wrote followed more or less completely the usage of the language spoken in their time, are nearly always of mediocre importance, most often insignificant, beside those important changes which have taken place without being noted by anyone. To determine the linguistic states of the past, the linguist must make use of the most exact, the most precise philology ; and each advance in philological precision permits a new advance for the linguist. The closer and closer contact which has fortunately been established between philologists and comparatists is necessary for the linguist to be able to utilize all the facts, sure data, and facts observed with the utmost precision. But by itself philology does not bring even a beginning of linguistic history.

Comparison is the only effective tool which the linguist has at his disposal to write the history of languages. We observe the results of changes, not the changes themselves. It is thus only with the aid of combinations that we follow — and can follow — linguistic development.

But these combinations are, as we shall see, rigorous and precise. All rest on the affirmation that certain agreements between different languages cannot be explained by features common to all men and require the hypothesis of a particular tradition.

Such is the essence of the comparative method. In order to estimate the conclusive value of a combination, we must only never lose sight of this characteristic of the proof.

II.

COMMON LANGUAGES

From the fact that the comparative method is the only one which permits us to do linguistic history it follows that as long as a language is isolated, it has no history. Between the state of Basque in the sixteenth century and the state of Basque today, there are differences ; but the changes are not essential ; in substance, the language has remained the same. If, therefore, one did not find any means of relating Basque to another language, there would not be any hope of ever reconstructing its history. However, if the attempts made by Marr and Oštir on the one hand, and Trombetti on the other, to relate Basque to a large group of languages of the Mediterranean basin and especially to the Caucasian languages succeed, then Basque will leave its isolation and enter history.

For all the groups now established and studied in a proper manner, the way to make a comparison is to posit an initial « common language » (German *Ursprache*). It means nothing to posit only partial comparisons : each linguistic fact is part of a system where everything holds together. We must not compare one fact of detail with another fact of detail, but one linguistic system with another system. Clearly, it is not always possible to reconstruct in this way a whole language by comparative methods ; we cannot even affirm a priori that it is necessary in all cases to reconstruct a single initial language — the problem of « mixed » languages will be considered later. But when it succeeds completely, comparison succeeds in reconstructing an initial language.

What is the value of this reconstruction ? It is almost never possible to compare the reconstruction with a known reality. But there is one case where we can ; it is that of the Romance languages. The common language to which we are led by comparison of the Romance languages does not furnish — far from it — everything that Latin was at the moment when the languages which continue Latin separated from each other. If we knew of Latin only what the Romance languages show, we would not know, for example, the old future of the type *amabo* or of the type *dicam*, *dices*. And above all we would have no idea of the declension : down to the thirteenth century, the Gallo-Romance dialects distinguish a subject case from an object case in the masculine ; the other Romance dialects do not even make this distinction. The Romance substantive is invariable in each number everywhere from the end of the thirteenth century. At the time when the Roman Empire was dissolved, declension survived and still played a great role. If comparison furnishes data which agree with attested reality in many regards — as for the verbal inflection, it is far from furnishing the whole language. Certain survivals, curious for whoever possesses the old form, would be unintelligible for the linguist who made use of comparison alone : the nasal of Fr. *rien* appears as a remnant of the old accusative when we know that the Latin accusative was characterized by the ending *-m* ; but the Romanist who utilized comparison alone would not have any means of recognizing there an accusative like Lat. *rem*. « Reconstruction » thus furnishes an incomplete idea, and without doubt generally a very incomplete idea, of the « common language ».

The languages which continue the same « common language » do not merely preserve certain old features of it. For a long time they preserve a tendency to show either identical or similar innovations, in such a way that certain parts of the « common language » disappear everywhere without leaving traces, or only leave traces impossible to discern if one did not know in fact the « common language ».

In all the Romance languages the declension of nouns, which was an element so essential to old Latin, was eliminated early. The elimination took place in an independent way in each language ; the Gallo-Romance dialects bear witness to this, since after having preserved a remnant of the declension in the form of an opposition between a subject case and an

object case, they in turn lost this survival by the end
of the thirteenth century.

Everywhere in the Romance languages the final
nasal of the old accusative was lost : French has no
trace of the final nasal of *terram* or of *regem* in its
forms *terre*, *roi*. This nasal was preserved only in the
accented monosyllable *rem* which became Fr. *rien*.

But if profound and numerous parallel innovations
prevent the reconstruction of comparatists from being
very complete, there is a correctness at the basis of
the reconstruction. Thus the constancy with which final
-*m* is noted in classical Latin orthography does not
give an exact notion of the reality. This final nasal
was weakly pronounced. In the oldest Latin the
orthography often does not denote it. For the poets,
a final -*m* does not prevent elision before a vowel :
in Latin prosody -*am* of *terram* is elided before a
vowel exactly as -*a* of *terra*. The absence of final -*m*
in the Romance languages indicates the weakness of
this nasal in Latin, a weakness which classical Latin
orthography conceals.

Moreover, for a person who intends to study the
Romance languages, the features of Latin which
disappeared without trace are not very important.
What are useful to him are the elements which served
to establish the new forms taken by Latin. Reconstruction does not furnish real Latin as it was spoken ;
and no reconstruction could furnish the « common
language » as it was spoken. It was a daring feat of
genius for Schleicher to « reconstruct » Indo-European

with the aid of the historically attested languages of
the family ; but it was a grave error on his part to
compose a text in this reconstructed language. Comparison brings a system of equations on which the history
of a family of languages can be based ; it does not
furnish a real language with all the means of expression which this language had.

Between the initial « common language » reconstructed by comparison and a language attested in fact,
one or more intermediate « common languages » can
be interposed. Thus, between Indo-European and the
Romance languages there is an important « common
language » — « Common Romance », which is conven-
tionally termed « Vulgar Latin ». Likewise, between
Indo-European and Gothic, Old High German, Old
English, and Old Norse, there was a « common language » — « Common Germanic », a language not in
fact attested, but whose existence is assumed by a set
of systematic innovations. These stages much facilitate the explanation.

If Romanists had to go back to Common Indo-
European to explain the facts of French, Italian,
Spanish, Portuguese, and Rumanian and did not
possess the « Common Romance » stage, the explanation of the facts would remain singularly incomplete,
most often impossible.

When such stages are not made use of, serious
difficulties are encountered. This is what happens to
Romanists when they encounter local Gallo-Romance
or Italian dialects. There was no « Common Gallo-

Romance » or « Common Italian ». One must thus compare each Gallo-Romance or Italian dialect with Common Romance without an intermediate stage. This does not mean that the dialects of northern France, for example, did not have many features, the most characteristic of which are found in literary French based on the dialect of Paris. But since the time of separation of the Romance dialects, each has had its own history. The Romanists who are concerned with Gallo-Romance dialects and Italian dialects are thus obliged either to reconstruct for each dialect the entire history of the type to which the dialect studied belongs or to employ simplifications which are to a certain degree arbitrary. To get out of this difficulty, diverse attemps have been made, notably that of Oscar Bloch concerning the dialects of a region of the Vosges (that of Remiremont). Whatever ingenuity is used to escape the difficulty, it is not possible to avoid it completely.

When we make use of intermediate common languages, the explanation of the facts is very much facilitated. But it is not always possible to make full use of them. Thus between Indo-European and Latin, it is known that there were two periods of unity : an Italo-Celtic period and an Italic period (« Italic » having furnished Latin and Osco-Umbrian). But the period of Italo-Celtic unity is of little use because it was of too short duration to produce numerous and profound innovations. And the period of Italic unity is of scarcely more use because Osco-

Umbrian is known only in a very fragmentary way.

For each language the problem of the reconstruction of the initial « common language » is an individual one. It is necessary in each case to make use of the special circumstances which present themselves.

« Common language » implies common civilization. For there is in fact a common language only where a dialect is extended to domains where it was not used before. It may happen that this common language brought by conquerors or colonists is never accepted by the old native population and that the latter emigrates or disappears : such is in general the case of English in North America. It may happen also that the people who bring the new language mix with the natives and that the natives accept the new language in spite of the small number of invaders : such is the case of Spanish or of Portuguese in certain parts of Central and South America. In all cases, a language spreads only if it is the organ of a civilization endowed with prestige. And it even happens that the spread of a language is entirely due to the prestige of a civilization : the Attic-Ionic *koinē* replaced all the other Greek dialects because it was the organ of the Hellenic civilization *par excellence*.

If Latin was accepted in the whole western part of the Roman Empire, it is because it brought with it a civilization superior to that of the peoples subjugated by Rome. In the eastern part of the Empire, where Greek served a civilization more ancient and, at least from the intellectual point of view, superior, Latin did not win out. In Gaul, the aristocracy began to study Latin after the conquest, and from the beginnings of the imperial period it was completely of Latin culture. Gaulish did not, however, disappear ; the people still preserved its usage for a long time. The artisans of the Gaulish pottery factory recently explored in southern France still used Gaulish ; the grammar they used was Gaulish ; the numerals were Gaulish ; but everything pertaining to civilization was already no longer Gaulish : the male proper names are not Gaulish ; nor are the names for the vases manufactured (see the remarks of J. Vendryes on this subject, *Bulletin de la Société de linguistique*, XXV, pp. 39 ff.). It is the prestige of a superior civilization which induces a people to change its language.

This superiority is not necessarily of a material nature. It may consist of a social organization particularly adapted to the needs of a given period and region. There is no reason to believe that the nation whose language was « Common Indo-European » had at its disposal material means superior to those of its neighbors, that it was, for example, more advanced in agriculture or in metallurgy. What characterizes the old Indo-European peoples is their sense of social organization and the power of initiative of their aristocracy. This organization did not have central power. Each family head was master in his extended family. Each tribal chief was independent of the others. At the very most there were temporary and

unstable federations. Everywhere that the old Indo-European peoples are observed, we see autonomous tribes and families where the authority is exercised by a *pater familias*. Each Greek city is a small independent State, just as each Gaulish or Germanic group. As soon as a chief feels capable of grouping around him enterprising men, he departs for whatever region in which he can find the means to lead his own autonomous life. The colonization of the Mediterranean shores by the ancient Greeks like that of Iceland, England, Normandy, and as far as Sicily by the Vikings — S. Bugge, with his sharp intuition of reality has already related the two movements — are illustrious examples of this spirit of independence and adventure. The Indo-European nation was thus composed of small groups who must have kept a sense of their unity for a long time and who, even after the time when the general unity of the Indo-European world had dissolved, formed nations of the same type which also had their own unity. For example, the Indo-Iranian group, whose native name is *ắrya-*, spread widely over Asia : we perceive it in the thirteenth century in Cappadocia, and the Assyro-Babylonians assumed contact with it in Media. The « Aryan » nation pushed its conquests far ahead to the Iranian plateau, to India, to the whole southern shore of the Black Sea, and to the East to the borders of China, where some Sogdian texts dating from the beginning of the Christian era were found near the Great Wall.

In thus dispersing and carrying from the extremities of Asia to the extremities of Europe their type of social organization with their language, the Indo-European peoples lost their sense of old national unity and their linguistic unity. The new groups which were established on each of the domains occupied lost in turn their unity. The Aryan world, the Germanic world, and the Celtic world were dislocated as was the Indo-European world. One has come in this way to the modern world where almost every country has its « common language », and where this common language is tending to obliterate the local dialects. There is here a new state of things which cannot ultimately endure : the proliferation of « common languages » in the Europe of today at a time when there is basically a unity of material and intellectual civilization is an anomaly.

Each of the great « common languages » of the past must express a type of civilization. And it is for this reason that the majority of the languages of the world appear to go back to a restricted number of common languages As long as the different comparative grammars are not established, nothing can be affirmed absolutely. But we already have the impression in particular that all the Negro languages of Africa rest on the same original language. It would be hazardous to place linguistic areas in an exact, constant, and regular relation to areas of civilization. But a connection is certain. And it will be one of the tasks of the study of man in the future to connect the common languages with areas of civilization. Already we have an indication of characteristic agreements.

III.

PROOFS

To establish the existence of an ancient common language, it is necessary to find in the languages compared the specific features of that language as far as they have been maintained. It is thus necessary to seek how the different elements of language behave ; for they are not preserved equally nor in the same way. Every language has three distinct systems which are connected with each other in definite ways, but are capable of varying to a great extent independently of each other : morphology, phonology, and vocabulary.

Morphology, that is, the set of processes by which words are modified and grouped to form sentences, is the most stable thing in language. But it is necessary to distinguish here between the general processes and the specific details of the forms.

Considered in a general way, morphological types are not very different. The principal difference consists in the fact that in certain languages relations between words and the various uses of words are marked by special forms which the words themselves

assume, while in other languages relations and uses
are marked by additional elements, by particles or
accessory words, and by word order. In the first group
of languages, there is what is called inflection. Yet
this distinction is not absolute, and there are mixtures
of the various processes in differing amounts.

Although the usage made of some type is often
maintained for a very long time and leaves traces
even when the type as a whole tends to be abolished,
one may not make use of these general types at all
to prove a « genetic relationship ». For it often
happens that with time the type tends to die out
more or less completely, as appears from the history
of the Indo-European languages.

Common Indo-European presented in the most
extreme way the type which is called « inflectional ».
All uses of words and all connections between words
were marked by differences in the internal form of
the words. In Sanskrit, where this nature of « Common Indo-European » is particularly well preserved,
« I am » is *ásmi*, « they are » is *sánti*, « he was » is
ása, and so forth. If the word « father » is subject,
it has the form *pitá* ; if it is direct object, it has the
form *pitáram* ; and if it is the complement of a noun,
it has the form *pitúh*. We see that the differences are
profound between the forms of the same word ; and
it is by means of these differences that the whole
role of the words is indicated. Up to the present
time even the most evolved languages of the Indo-
European family have preserved something of this

old type ; in French, for example, the substantive has become invariable (the -*s* of the plural is purely graphic) ; but the verb has still much inflection : the difference between *aime* and *aimez*, *j'aimais* and *nous aimions* is characteristic, and even more that between *je veux*, *nous voulons*, *je voudrais*, *j'ai voulu*, etc. Nevertheless, the general structure of modern French differs completely from that which Indo-European had. And the structure of English differs even more. The Romance languages, the majority of Germanic languages, and the Iranian languages no longer really merit today the name « inflectional ». And even the most conservative Indo-European languages have a type completely different from Common Indo-European. The structures of the various Indo-European languages spoken today are very different from the structure which Common Indo-European had and, besides, are very different from each other. Consequently, it is not by its general structure that an Indo-European language is recognized.

The « Common Indo - European » process was suffixation, that is, the grammatical elements affixed to the part of the word expressing the meaning were always placed behind. So in Latin, where this usage is well preserved, the mark -*ēs* of the nominative and accusative plural and the mark -*um* of the genitive plural are placed after *patr-* : *patr-ēs* « fathers », *patr-um* « of the fathers ». In French, on the other hand, there is a tendency for prefixes to be formed. Latin distinguished *amō*, *amās*, *amat* by the end of

the word. French distinguishes *j'aime, tu aimes*
(with purely graphic *-s*), *il aime* by the elements *je,
tu, il* which traditional grammar calls « pronouns »,
but which do not have any autonomous existence
and are now pure grammatical signs placed in front.
Again in this regard, the French process is different
from that of Indo-European.

Thus it is not with such general features of structure, which are subject to change completely in the
course of several centuries and moreover do not have
very numerous variations, that one can establish
linguistic relationships. Anyone who compared Latin,
where we have *liber Petri* or *Petri liber* (both orders
are possible), that is, where the relation between
« Peter » and « book » is marked by the form *Petri*
of the noun whose nominative is *Petrus*, and whose
accusative is *Petrum*, etc., with variations at the end
of the word, and French, where the relation between
the noun and its complement is indicated by the
particle *de* placed in front and by the position of *de
Pierre*, would not find any common feature between
the processes used by the two languages.

What conclusively establish the continuity between
one « common language » and a later language are
the particular processes of expression of the morphology. For example, it is not uncommon that the
relation of dependence between two substantives is
expressed by a particle either placed in front like
Fr. *de* or placed behind like Eng. *-s*. But the fact
that this particle has the form *de* or the form *-s* is

characteristic ; for any other speech sound could indicate the relation equally well, had not the tradition decided otherwise. Consequently, the fact that the relation is marked by *de* placed in front of the complement is a distinctive characteristic of French, and the fact that the relation is marked by -*s* placed after the complement is a distinctive characteristic of English. One must add that the use of *de* may disappear from a French dialect or that of -*s* from an English dialect without these dialects ceasing to be French or English. Only positive facts have a conclusive value.

Singular facts of this sort are often stable. The pronunciation can be transformed and the vocabulary can change, while these features remain. Thus in the modern dialects of northern France, the local forms of words are being modified to conform to French forms, the vocabulary is being renewed, and there is a general tendency to speak according to Common French usage. What survive in the final analysis are local morphological peculiarities, like the mark of the masculine and feminine by *i dit*, *a dit*, where Common French has *il dit*, *elle dit*. Specific facts of this sort are learned from infancy ; they become habits of which one is not aware and are capable of remaining when everything else is modified.

Consequently, a language with an involved and complex morphology, containing a large number of specific facts, lends itself well to the proof of relationships, whereas a language with a simple morphology, operating principally with general processes such as word order, makes the discovery of valid proofs difficult. One has hardly need of proving that a language is Indo-European : everywhere that an unknown Indo-European language has been found, such as Tocharian or Hittite in recent times, its Indo-European character has been revealed at the very beginning of its decipherment and interpretation. On the other hand, languages of the Far East like Chinese or Annamese, which hardly show special morphological traits, do not even have anything which the linguist who attempts to find languages related to the Chinese or Annamese dialects may cling to ; and the reconstruction of a « common language » of which Chinese, Tibetan, etc., for example, would be later forms, comes up against obstacles all but invincible.

The more singular the facts are by which the agreement between two languages is established, the greater is the conclusive force of the agreement. Anomalous forms are thus those which are most suited to establish a « common language ».

The fact that French *il est, ils sont, je fus* agree with Latin *est, sunt, fui* is such to make it clear that French is a new form taken by Latin. Agreements like *je veux, nous voulons, je voulus* with *uolō, uolumus, uoluī* or like *je dis, nous disons, dit* with *dīcō, dīcimus, dictus* confirm the proof. The « irregular » verbs thus bring a multitude of means of proof.

The adjective confirms the proof. Here we observe, in fact, the distinction between a masculine and a feminine, whose use is arbitrary, when it does not depend on sex. This distinction devoid of meaning is found in both French and Latin : *veston neuf* and *veste neuve*, just as Latin has *nouus, noua*. It even is clear from certain forms, the article *la*, and the possessive adjectives *ma, ta, sa*, that the feminine is sometimes characterized by *a* both in French and in Latin.

Thus the more a language contains non-meaningful grammatical categories or anomalous forms, the easier the proof of relationships and the reconstruction of an initial common language are for the linguist.

The initial linguistic unity is not always recognized by a retention pure and simple ; it is often shown by divergent innovations. Thus Indo-European had a certain type of verbal inflection of complicated form which tended to be eliminated everywhere ; its original presence may be recognized from innovations which vary from one language to another. For example, there was a present of the form **eiti* « he goes », **y-enti* or **iy-enti*, **y-onti* or **iy-onti* « they go » ; Sanskrit preserves it in the form *éti, yánti ;* Attic Greek has it, a little more altered, in *eisi, iāsi ;* Latin, with even more alteration, in *it, eunt ;* old Lithuanian has the singular *eiti ;* but these forms were too singular : modern Lithuanian has replaced *eiti* by a formation of a new type regular in Lithuanian, *eina ;* Slavic has from the ninth century A.D.,

in the language of the ancient translators, *idetŭ* « he goes », *idǫtŭ* « they go ». The new forms of Lithuanian, *einu* « I go », and of Slavic, *idǫ*, reflect in their way the original form which was eliminated.

In the example cited, the original form is preserved by certain languages, and the innovation of certain others can be easily explained. But it happens that the original form is nowhere preserved, and it is only the absence of agreement of detail of the forms compared which permits the positing of a singular form eliminated later. There must have been in Indo-European a present of the form *melǝti* and *molǝti* « he grinds » with a third person plural *mᵒlenti* and *mᵒlonti*. This difficult inflection was eliminated everywhere. Nevertheless, its ancient existence is recognized in the fact that Slavic has *meljetŭ*, Lithuanian *malu* and Gothic *malip*, Irish *melid* and all the neighboring Brittonic languages a form with different vocalism, *mal-*, etc. Nowhere are the Indo-European forms posited here preserved ; but they may be reconstructed from the knowledge which we have of the Indo-European system and by the divergences observed among the languages historically known.

The observation of singular facts does not excuse one from examining the whole of the morphology. Every morphology constitutes a complete system. From the set of agreements, it is thus necessary to reconstruct the system of the « common language », as far as is possible. And after this is done, it is necessary to see how to this system are opposed the morphological systems — often completely different, as has been seen — of the languages into which the initial language was transformed. Particular features are the decisive means of proof. But the proof is not definitively established until one has confronted morphological system with morphological system and until one has seen how it is possible to pass from the initial system to the later systems.

Then it is often observed that the general characteristics of the ancient system are maintained for a long time. Thus in Common Indo-European, where each word contained in itself the mark of its role in the sentence, the noun was clearly distinguished from the verb. Still today in the Indo-European languages, the distinction between the noun and the verb has remained clear everywhere.

Phonology involves also relating an ancient system to new systems, all these systems being able to differ from each other as profoundly as is imaginable.

But the differences between one system and another are not capricious. If it is often impossible to recognize regular correspondences between two languages derived from a common original, the correspondences between the common language and each of these languages obey fixed rules which can be exactly formulated. It is these which are called « phonetic laws ».

To Indo-European p, t, k correspond f, p, x (whence h) in Germanic and, under certain conditions, b, d,

Υ ; to Indo-European *b*, *d*, *g* correspond Gmc. *p*, *t*, *k* ; to Indo-European *bh*, *dh*, *gh* correspond Gmc. *b*, *d*, *g* (*ƀ*, *đ*, *Ɣ* in intervocalic position). This regular system of correspondences in Germanic is what is called the « consonant shift » or Grimm's Law (seen in large part by Rask a little before Grimm, but posited as a law by Grimm). The regularity of the correspondences between the initial « common language » and the later languages expresses the fact that the changes in pronunciation do not affect some word or some form in isolation, but affect the phonological system itself.

From the principle of the method it results that rules of correspondences can be posited between the initial language and each of the languages which continue it, but not between the different languages continuing the same common language. It can be posited that initial Indo-European *p* is represented in Greek and Sanskrit by *p*, in Gothic by *f*, as in Gr. *patér*, Skr. *pitá*, and Goth. *fadar* « father », and that initial Indo-European *kʷ* before *o* is represented in Greek by *p*, in Sanskrit by *k*, and in Gothic by *hw*, as Gr. *póteros*, Skr. *kataráḥ*, Goth. *hwapar* « which of two ». The two correspondences established :

Gr. *p* = Skr. *p* = Goth. *f*

Gr. *p* = Skr. *k* = Goth. *hw*

are in fact intelligible only in relation to a Common Indo-European form posited to explain them.

It is not with similarities of forms that we work when we compare languages of the same family, but solely with rules of correspondences. We have seen above, p. 18, that the Armenian numeral « two », *erku*, corresponds to Proto-Indo-European **dwō* (or **duwō*). This correspondence seems strange at first sight. But there is a general rule by virtue of which Armenian *erk-* corresponds to Indo-European *dw-*. For two other examples of this correspondence are known. Indo-European had a root **dwei-* « to fear », which is widely represented in Homeric Greek by verbal forms such as **dedwoa* (written *deidō*), *dedwoike* (written *deidoike*) « I fear » or nominal forms such as **dweos* (written *deos*) « fear » ; Armenian *erkiwl* « fear », *erkeay* « I feared » correspond to them. There was an adjective **dwāro-* « long », preserved specifically by Greek ; Armenian has an adjective *erkar* « long ». The rule is thus based on three evident equations. If one thinks of the restricted number of known Indo-European words having initial **dw-*, **duw-*, the coexistence of these three equations is clearly convincing.

The correspondence can in fact be explained. The group of dental consonant followed by *w* becomes a velar in Armenian : *tw-* is represented by *k'-*, as in *k'o* « of you », in face of such Greek forms as *twe* (whence Attic *se*). The voiceless *k* comes from the fact that there was a shift of the old voiced stops to voiceless stops both in Armenian and in Germanic : *d* goes to *t*, *g* to *k*. The *r* which precedes is a trace of the old voiced character of the initial consonant of the group (for details of the explanation, see **Gram-**

mont, *Mémoires de la Soc. de ling.*, XX, p. 252) ;
this r has produced in turn the development of the
initial e which figures in *erku*. The presence of -*r*-
in the interior of the word, moreover, sufficed to
prevent the development of initial r : *kr-kin* is the
word which means « double » (*krkin* rests on an old
*kir-kin or **kurkin*). Everything in the very strange
correspondence of Arm. *erk-* with **dw-* results from
the structure of Armenian. A correspondence which
could not be explained in such a way would be
suspect.

In groups of languages where we have long series
of clear equations and whose belonging to the same
family is consequently not in question, we can utilize
surprising correspondences such as that of Arm. *erk-*
in face of **dw-*, **duw-* of the other languages of the
group and can posit Arm. *erk(i)-* = Lat. *bi-*, as
strange as this appears at first sight. It goes without
saying that one cannot make use of such correspondences to begin to establish a language family. One is
obliged to begin with equations whose explanation is
readily apparent.

The regularity of correspondences does not exclude
the existence of special treatments. In a sentence
words are found in various positions and under various
conditions. The regularity of treatment comes often
from the fixture of a median form among those
varying according to the position in the sentence. But
there are in particular cases where forms pronounced
more rapidly or carelessly are more usual than others,

and from this result special treatments of accessory words : a reduction like that of *hiu tagu* « this day » to *hiutu* (mod. Ger. *heute*) in Old High German enters into no general category.

These phenomena which cannot be reduced to general formulas cause no difficulty in a language whose history is known and for which we possess well established rules of correspondences. It is superfluous to note that in a language whose history is not established in an exact way facts so aberrant are not utilizable and that it is appropriate to disregard them temporarily.

As far as vocabulary is concerned, it is the most unstable element of all in language. Words are subject to disappear for the most varied reasons ; they are replaced by new terms. To the native vocabulary can also be added new words as much and more numerous than the old ones : thus upon the Germanic vocabulary of English has been superimposed a Latin and French element as considerable as that of Germanic. It even happens that the whole vocabulary belongs to a group other than that on which the morphology is dependent : Gypsy Armenian has a morphology and a phonology wholly Armenian and a vocabulary wholly Gypsy.

Even when they survive, words are susceptible of changing their meaning so strongly that in spite of the antiquity of their form they are really new words. The Indo-European noun for the Indo-European head of family, *pǝter-*, has survived in French ; it is the word *père*. But whereas the Indo-European word designated a social role, and one could call the supreme god **pəter* as the most important family head, the French word designates more and more « he who begets » and passes to the meaning of Lat. *genitor*, almost to the meaning of « male » : one says of a male rabbit that he is a *père*. Thus Fr. *père* continues an Indo-European word, but with a value so different from the Indo-European value that it is really a new word.

In spite of this frequent instability of vocabulary, it is the agreements in vocabulary which are immediately striking when languages are compared to each other. Often one makes use only of vocabulary, either because the languages considered are not well known and one has information only on the vocabulary, or because it is a matter of languages with a very simple grammar as in the Far East, or because the morphological systems which have survived were established rather late, after the period of presumed unity. Thus it is very important to examine how an agreement in vocabulary can be proved.

It has already been noted that valid etymological comparisons are never made according to similarities in phonological form, but only according to rules of correspondences : if one can relate Arm. *erku* to Russian *dva*, it is not because the two forms resemble each other : the phonological forms have nothing in common ; it is because rules of correspondences permit the comparison. Indo-European *ō* going to *a* in Slavic and to *u* in Armenian, and Indo-European *duw-* going to *dv-* in Russian and to *erk-* in Armenian.

To the extent that they cannot be explained by conditions proper to this or that word, irregularities in correspondences reveal either a borrowing from other languages or an etymology to be discarded. An old Latin *ca-* is represented in French by *cha-*, *che-*, *chè-*, as in *campum* becoming *champ*, *carrum* becoming *char*, *caballum* becoming *cheval*, *carum* becoming *cher*, etc. ; if, therefore, one has *camp* in face of *campum*, it is because the word does not belong to the old French tradition ; in fact, it comes from Italian, and it is indeed known when and why it was « borrowed ». A *b-* in Germanic corresponds to a Latin *f- ;* we have, for example, *flōs*, *flōris* in Latin and *blume* in German ; consequently, German *feuer* has no connection with French *feu ;* it is sufficient, besides, to think of the Romance correspondents of Fr. *feu*, that is, It. *fuoco*, Sp. *fuego* for the resemblance of *feu* and *feuer* to disappear. Comparisons are thus made only with precise formulas of correspondences — and taking care to avoid what is due to borrowings.

Unfortunately, it is difficult to determine a priori what may be native and what may be borrowed. Verbs and adjectives are more often native than substantives : verbs like *vivre* and *mourir*, *venir* and *dormir* of modern French are still Indo-European verbs, and likewise adjectives like *vif*, *vieux*, *neuf*, etc. Nevertheless, a strong verb like Ger. *schreiben* is borrowed from Lat. *scribere*. On the other hand, many French substantives such as *pied, chien, veuve*, etc. are Indo-European. The risk that a word is borrowed is always great, and the etymologist of an ancient or modern language who reasons as if the words to be explained had a priori every chance of being native exposes himself to frequent errors.

When it is a matter of words really going back to the « common language », it is necessary to recon-struct a word of this language which is defined in every respect, and not to be content with comparing small root elements. And as the risks of error are great, it is necessary to assure oneself precisely that the agreements observed are not fortuitous.

The first point, on which one is in agreement in fact if not in principle, is that an etymology is valid only if the rules of phonological correspondences are applied in an exact way, or, in case a divergence is accepted, if this divergence is explained by special circumstances rigorously defined.

It goes without saying that the larger the number of phonological elements which correspond to each other, the smaller the risk that the agreement is fortuitous.

Chance can obviously not cause that « widow » be *vidhávā* in Sanskrit, *vidova* in Slavic, *widdewū* in Old Prussian, *widuwo* in Gothic, *fedb* in Irish, *uidua* in Latin, it being given, for example, that Irish *f* and Latin *u-* (consonant) correspond to initial *v* of Sanskrit. The agreement of *w, i, dh*, and *u*, in this order, cannot be accidental. Between the Sanskrit, Slavic, and Prussian forms, and the Germanic, Irish, and doubtless Latin forms, there is, it is true, a difference : the presence of a vowel *e* (or *o*) between *dh* and *w* in the first group of languages and the absence of this vowel in the other ; this difference does not cause any difficulty ; for it is dependent on vocalic alternations known from Indo-European.

But if instead of thus comparing four phonological elements exactly corresponding to each other, we compared only three, the proof is less valid, and it becomes weak if we make use of only two concordant elements and almost non-existent if we make use of one element alone. Thus linguists who work with small root elements and who even often analyze roots to compare no more than fragments of roots thereby ruin in advance the proof which they seek. A comparison of complete words having some extent can be sure. A comparison which rests solely on one or even two root consonants is without value if it is not supported by very specific facts.

The agreement in meaning should be as exact and as precise as the agreement in phonological form (according to the rules of correspondence). This does not mean that the meanings should coincide more than the phonological elements ; only the differences in the meanings, if there are any, should be explained, not by vague and general possibilities, but by special circumstances. The fact that Fr. *ouaille* rests on Lat. *ouicula* is not made doubtful by the fact that in modern French this word designates only the congregation of the priest of some church. But the comparison is justified because it is known that the congregation of a Christian church is generally compared to a flock which the pastor of this church tends. Moreover, in local French dialects the word *ouaille* is found in the meaning of « sheep », which finishes proving the correctness of the etymology.

Concerning Indo-European etymology, the fact that words have varied inflections furnishes decisive confirmations. Take, for example, the word which signifies « sheep » (male or female : Indo-European had no distinct names for animals with respect to sex) : Sanskrit *áviḥ*, Greek *óis* (thus in Homer), Latin *ouis*, Lithuanian *avis* ; the agreement in meaning and form among all these languages is perfect ; and, as one succeeds in thus reconstructing a word well defined by its phonological form and meaning, the etymology can be considered as already certain. But there is added the fact that the two languages earliest attested, those which are thus suited for giving the most correct idea of certain details of Indo-European facts, have an inflection of special type : the Sanskrit genitive-ablative *ávyaḥ* agrees exactly with Greek *oiós*, which rests on *owyós. In the other languages, the inflection has been normalized, as one expects. But Sanskrit and Greek inflect the word in the same way. This is a supplementary precision which succeeds in excluding chance and adds to the rigor of the proof.

When one must reconstruct an initial « common

language », one should take account of the number of pieces of evidence which there are for a given word. An agreement of two languages, if it is not complete, risks being fortuitous. But if the agreement is extended to three, four, or five very different languages, chance becomes less likely. Although Old Persian *rādiy* « on account of » and Slavic *radi* « on account of » are not found elsewhere, one does not hesitate to relate the two words because form, meaning, and details of use agree in every way. Apart from a case of this type, a comparison of words found in only two Indo-European languages is suspect unless one can recognize the special conditions which caused the elimination of the word in the other languages.

Whatever language is concerned, an etymology can be considered as proved only if a set of precise agreements establishes that the similarities of the words compared cannot be due to chance.

Every word does not have the right to an etymology, as sometimes might be believed in going through etymological dictionaries. The rule of method is that only well determined positive facts justify a comparison : the proof that chance is excluded is the burden of the etymologist. This proof can be administered in various ways according to languages and circumstances ; the conditions vary from one language to another and from one word to another. But it is always necessary that the proofs be precise and rigorous.

The number of good etymologies is also rather

restricted, at least for the languages whose history is known only by comparison and where the comparative method does not find in series of texts of different periods the support of precise historical evidence. When one reads a manual of comparative grammar, one is struck at once by finding it based on a small number of comparisons. This is because there are few of them on which it is permitted to make a foundation without reservation.

A language like Indo-European, where the words are most often at least dissyllabic or trisyllabic and where the inflections are varied and complex, lends itself well to perfect etymological proofs (one can neglect the more or less laborious fantasies of the linguists who are content with inferiority). Likewise Semitic, with its roots which normally contain three consonants, permits perfect etymologies. On the other hand, the languages where the words are short, often monosyllabic, and do not have special inflections exclude by their structure rigorous etymological proofs. It will be necessary to find a new method for these if one wishes to arrive at real proofs.

We have considered here only etymologies made by comparison between different languages and going back to a word of the initial common language. To determine in what way the history of all the words can be reconstructed — which is outside the field of these lectures —, a long study would be necessary which would consider methods of all sorts.

For example, there are some words which can be

explained, within a given language, by processes of formation proper to this language. A noun like Greek *(w)érgon* « work » finds an etymology by comparison with German *werk* and by the observation that the form of this word is normal in Indo-European, the root being found also in Armenian and Iranian. But to explain Greek *órganon* « instrument », it is necessary to consider a productive suffix which has furnished many other nouns in Greek.

There are many words whose history can be explained only by factual data : thus Latin *organum* is explicable only if it is known that the technical vocabulary of Latin is in large part Greek or an imitation of Greek. And if there are two representatives of this word in French, *orgue* and *organe*, with meanings which have nothing in common, this results from special conditions ; if these conditions are known, it is because it is a matter of facts having taken place during historical periods ; no comparative method would permit one to discover them.

In fact, the largest part of the etymology of words eludes the comparative method and is dependent on history reconstructed with the aid of evidence. When the evidence is lacking, and when one cannot follow, by making use of positive and precise data, the accidents which have happened to a word, it is most often vain to attempt to give a true etymology of it.

Whether it is a question of morphology, phonology,

or vocabulary, the principle which must never be lost sight of is that comparisons are valid only to the degree that they are subjected to strict rules. The more freedom the linguist gives himself, the more arbitrary are his comparisons and the more precarious his proofs. For example, the linguist who interprets the proper names of a country by comparisons with a language which is supposed to be related to the one which was spoken in this country before a change of language plays a dangerous game. If one is sure of the language which was formerly spoken and if one knows well languages quite closely related to it, some explanations of this type are sure : a Gallo-Romance locality called *Brīua* (*Brive*) has certainly a Gaulish name because it is at a point where a bridge must always have existed, because the Celtic languages preserved presuppose a noun *brīwā* for « bridge », and because Latin has taken the place of Gaulish, a language certainly Celtic, in the country where Brive is located. But it is hazardous to explain some Greek place name by a comparison with the Caucasian languages in a case where nothing indicates the sounds which the proper name in question should have etymologically, where the languages compared have an unidentical form, and where no historical data prove that a language closely related to the Caucasian languages was spoken. Generally, the etymologies of proper names are uncertain because of the two pieces of data whose value is established by agreement with the facts of other languages, meaning and phonological

form, we can utilize only one : phonological form.
The linguists who are especially interested in the
etymology of proper names are often linguistic adven-
turers, and few are those who have all the methodological requirements needed.

IV.

LINGUISTIC DEVELOPMENT
BETWEEN THE PERIOD OF UNITY
AND THE HISTORICAL PERIOD

Comparison permits us, to the degree indicated, to « reconstruct » the « common language » of which the languages of the same « family » are the forms taken in the course of time. But it remains to understand what happened between the period of « unity » and the date when the languages begin to be attested in fact. The problem is difficult, often insoluble.

It goes without saying that we must make use of the intermediate periods of unity which we can either determine exactly or perceive. We thus restrict as much as possible the importance of the interval between the « common language » and the attested languages. But, as has been seen on pp. 29 ff., these periods of unity do not always exist, or when they did exist, it is not always possible to make use of them or to make use of them for all the facts. Even in the best cases, the gap between the « common language » and the attested languages remains large, and the interpolations which are made to fill it up have much inexactitude and arbitrariness.

The consideration of linguistic facts is not sufficient to furnish even the beginning of a chronology. For the rapidity of linguistic changes varies to a great degree. Certain languages can remain for long centuries almost without change : known since the twelfth century, the Turkic dialects have preserved since then the same essential features, so that although sometimes separated from each other for a thousand years, they continue to be very similar to each other. Little is known of the history of the Polynesian dialects ; but what is striking is that in spite of the great distances which separate the islands of Polynesia from each other, these dialects have remained almost identical to each other. Cases of this type are not rare : the languages of not very civilized peoples often have a great stability.

The rapidity of change which is sometimes attributed to the languages of the half-civilized can be explained, at least in part, by usages relating to the vocabulary. It often happens among the half-civilized that words are tabooed ; for example, as a result of the death of an individual, the word which figures in his name is often forbidden. Consequently, the traveler who has known a given vocabulary can, if he returns some years later, find another different from it in many respects. Thalbitzer has recently made known a case of this type among Eskimos. But the result thereof is not a fundamental change in the language itself.

Elsewhere, on the other hand, rapid changes of the linguistic system are found. In the third and even in the fifth century A.D., Latin doubtless still had much of its ancient character, especially at first sight. In the ninth century the Romance languages already had their essential features ; and even the way in which the writers of the Merovingian period write Latin from the sixth century onwards often indicates that the principal changes were realized or about to be. Likewise, the rather profound change which made modern Armenian from old Armenian was realized between the fifth century at the earliest and the tenth century at the latest ; since then there has not been so profound a change in Armenian. In the sixth century B.C. Persian still had an archaic aspect ; in the first century of our era it already had a modern aspect, and it has undergone no change of comparable importance since then.

Time is thus only one of the conditions on which the importance of changes depends. Neither does a good state of preservation of the ancient usage prove that the time elapsed after the rupture of the initial unity is short, nor does an extensive change of forms presuppose a long interval of time And since linguistic facts do not furnish any other indication, one most often can say nothing, even approximately, of the time which innovations have required.

The degree of change of a language in relation to the « common language » is not recognizable by the date : among the Semitic languages, there are two which have preserved declension. One of these two is Akkadian of the beginning of the second millennium before Christ, the other is Arabic of the seventh century A.D. In languages attested well before Arabic, like Hebrew or Aramaic, the declension of nouns no longer exists.

If there are moments when linguistic change seems precipitate, this is largely due to the fact that there is a long period of preparation for the innovations. The realization of the change in many cases only manifests the end point of a long development.

One of the principal facts to which is due the passage from the ancient Indo-European type to the modern type of languages of the family is the loss of the pitch accent and of quantitative rhythm. In the ancient type, of which the Vedic and classical Greek texts still give a clear idea, the « tone » consisted of an elevation of the voice and did not serve as the rhythmical summit of the word ; it played a semantic role analogous to that which the tones, that is, the ascents and descents of the voice, play in the Chinese or Sudanese dialects. The rhythm rested entirely on the alternation of long and short syllables. The comparison of diverse languages shows that this type was Common Indo-European. This phonic type was eliminated everywhere, notably in Greek and in Latin in the imperial period. Rhythm ceased to be based on the alternation of short and long syllables ; some of the long syllables were shortened, or even all the vowels lost the opposition of short and long quantity. And the ancient tone became the center of the word, the rhythmical summit. Consequently, the word is « centered » differently than it was, and the whole pronunciation changes its character. When this transformation is accomplished, the ancient tonic syllable acquires a special importance, whereas the other elements of the word become relatively secondary. In the Romance languages we know that the treatment of the accented syllable differs fundamentally from that of the other syllables of the word. The change of Lat. *caballum* into Fr. *cheval*, essentially realized from the ninth century, is specifically French; but it is only a consequence of the elimination of quantitative rhythm and of the change in character of the ancient tone which took place during the imperial period of Latin and had really begun to some degree before the first written monuments of Latin, that is, before the third century B.C., as various circumstances indicate. The change of *caballum* into *cheval*, which happened rather quickly, is what is visible. The preparation for this change required long centuries and is not visible at all.

These periods of preparation existed in the whole Indo-European domain, nearly everywhere before the historical period, or outside of periods when the development is observable. The history of Greek and Latin gives an idea of what could have happened ; we must not judge everything by it ; for in the Indo-Iranian domain, for example, the development of rhythm seems to have been quite different. But on the whole, there were preparations of this type everywhere.

What is observed in general in the Indo-European languages is the result of abrupt changes consecutive to the periods of preparation, as a result of which the language presents a new aspect, different from the Indo-European type.

Nominal inflection tends to be eliminated in the whole Indo-European domain. This elimination was favored by the tendency of the end of the word to be reduced, from which it resulted that the characteristics of case forms, situated at the end of the word, progressively lost their clarity. But the essential thing is that case inflection was little by little replaced by other processes of expression. From before the historical period, case forms no longer sufficed to indicate local relations : if Latin has obligatorily a preposition in *eo in urbem, habito in urbe, uenio ex urbe*, this is not an isolated thing ; analogous facts are observed in the majority of the Indo-European languages from the beginning of the historical period, and the full value of the local cases was maintained only in more or less isolated survivals. Once this state was reached, case inflection became a superfluous complication, and it is not surprising that a language either restricted or suppressed it everywhere.

What makes it difficult, often impossible, to follow linguistic development between the period of unity and the historical periods is not only the difficulty of estimating the time which the change required, or the nearly invisible character of the periods of preparation for the changes.

There are many other causes of difficulty.

Later changes are largely governed by the state of

the common language and by the way in which it breaks
up. Consequently, identical or similar changes take
place even after the separation and the beginning of
the differentiation of the languages which are derived
from the « common language ». This fact is often unrec-
ognized. Treatises on comparative grammar often
proceed as if all the facts superimposable on the various
representatives of the same « common language » went
back to the period of unity. Doubtless the authors do not
believe this basically and certainly would avoid affirming it ; they sometimes even indicate reservations in
this respect. But the account is presented as if the
authors accepted such a hypothesis. Such is the case
notably for the remarkable *Grundriss* of Brugmann.
Nothing is less consistent with reality.

Take, for example, the characteristic -*m* of the first
person singular of verbs in the Slavic languages ; this
characteristic is found in a notable part of the conjugation in the majority of the modern Slavic languages,
and even in all the normal presents in Serbo-Croatian.
But in Common Slavic it was characteristic of four or
five anomalous verbs. Only in the course of the Middle
Ages at a historical date did the innovation take place,
notably in Czech and Serbo-Croatian. At this time the
Slavic languages had already been separated for a long
time, and each realized in an independent way the
innovation whose limits, in addition, vary from one
language to another.

Such facts are observed elsewhere for the same first
person singular : Armenian has also generalized a form

characterized by -*m*. Here we have only the result of the process, and the factual details by which Armenian arrived at it are lacking. In India and in Iran there was the same innovation, and we are almost completely ignorant of the way in which it arose. Fortunately, we possess a small series of old Iranian texts, the Gāthās of the Avesta, where the generalization of the ending -*mi* has not been made ; we see from this that although Sanskrit has a form *bhárāmi* for « I carry » and the Younger Avesta a form *barāmi*, the addition of -*mi* is later than the period of Indo-Iranian (Aryan) unity : for the Gāthās of the Avesta still have the type *barā*.

The agreements between the historically attested forms result, much more than we can imagine at first sight, from parallel developments in languages already separated and differentiated.

If similar creations are thus realized in a parallel way, but independently, certain ancient features are lost in a parallel way with even stronger reason. Owing to the fact that Greek still knows the famous rule *ta zōa trekhei* (coexistence of a singular verb with a subject in the neuter plural) in the classical period and that the same rule is found exactly observed in the Gāthās of the Avesta, we know that the form called « nomina-tive-accusative plural neuter » of Indo-European is in reality an ancient collective. But a language as archaic as Vedic already almost completely ignores it. Latin has generalized the use of the plural verb with a neuter plural subject ; Slavic, Celtic, and Germanic also. And even in Greek, the peculiarity was lost with time. When

we do not have very archaic forms of languages — and
this is the ordinary case — a large part of the events
of the intermediate period thus remain unknown.

But there are not only eliminations of ancient usages
and innovations of usages destined to endure. Linguistic
development is a complex thing, and we must not have
the illusion of explaining everything which was created
during intermediate periods or of reconstructing the
many events which took place during these periods.

We follow by means of texts the history of Greek
from the seventh century B.C. up to the present time,
and we have here an example which permits us to
judge the succession of creations and losses by which
the language arrived at its modern state.

Thus before the historical period Greek gave each
verb a future ; then in the Byzantine period it eliminated this future and replaced it with something completely new.

Greek had inherited one type of perfect : before and
during the historical period, it enlarged its use and
increased its forms ; it created processes whereby
nearly every verb could have a perfect. In the Attic
period the perfect was an essential form of the verb
and in general use. Then its usage disappeared, and
modern Greek no longer has any personal form of the
perfect.

Thus if we knew Greek as we know Slavic, only
from the beginning of the ninth century A.D., the
linguist could not even suspect that before arriving at
the present state of the verb with two stems, Greek

passed through a period when a future and a perfect had a rich development, that there were many creations, forms made and remade repeatedly : the linguist who knew only the end point would have no idea at all of this development.

The majority of the Indo-European languages are known only after the beginning of the Christian era, at a time when these complex developments which positive data permit us to observe in Greek were accomplished, and when, as a consequence, the linguist does not know what really happened.

It would be therefore fruitless to pretend to explain for certain all the new forms which were made between the period of unity and the historical periods. We should not be surprised that linguistics can make only weak and uncertain hypotheses concerning the origin of the Latin perfectum in -uī, the Greek perfect passive in -thēn, the Gothic preterite in -da (-ta), etc. These forms result from a development which took place during periods whose linguistic stage is not reconstructible ; the data are lacking for determining the details of the conditions whereby the innovations were realized. To wish to explain them at any price, to imagine that we can find here rigorous proofs is to lose sight of the limits of the comparative method.

Between the period of unity and the periods historically attested, there are developments not entirely reconstructible, which remain necessarily the more unknown the longer and, above all, the more filled with innovations the intermediate period is.

V.

DIALECTS

Hitherto we have considered the initial language and the historically attested languages as if they were as many unities. Such is not the case. The notion of « dialect », which recurs continually in linguistics, confirms this.

Here it is necessary to disregard the common meaning, which opposes « dialect » to an established literary language.

The word is Greek, and it was made for Greek situations. Ancient Greek is not a unity like Latin. It was written in different ways according to the time and the place. In one type of dialects the word for « island » is *nāsos*, and in another it is *nēsos* ; in one the dative plural is *possi, posi* « to the feet » and in another, *podessi* ; in one « I wish » is *boulomai*, in another, *bellomai*, and in a third, *dēlomai* ; in one « possession » is *ktēsis* and in another *p(p)āsis*. But these differences are not such that Greeks employing dialects of different types had the feeling of speaking distinct languages. Certain of these differences, like the opposition between *nēsos* and *nāsos*, enter into large groups of phonological correspondences, others like that between *podessi* and *possi, posi* are dependent on regular grammatical differences, still others are simple facts of vocabulary like *ktēsis : (p)pāsis*. These differences did not prevent the Greeks from feeling that they all had the same language on the whole. What characterizes the « dialect » first and foremost is, therefore, diversity in unity, unity in diversity.

The « dialect » itself is not a unity. The Greeks distinguished three great dialects: Ionic, Aeolic, and Doric, to which linguists of the present day add a fourth, Achaean (Arcado-Cypriote). But a given text is not written in one dialect ; there are different forms of each dialect. For example, there is no one form of Doric : there are Corinthian (with Syracusan), Argive, Laconian. Cretan, Rhodian, etc. And these general types admit of varieties : there is no one form of Cretan, and appreciable differences are observed between one locality of Crete and another; A « dialect » is a set of different local forms of speech which have common characteristics and are more similar to each other than they are to the other forms of speech of the same language.

Thirdly, the dialects do not necessarily embrace all the local forms of speech of a language. Thus in Greek, the most well-known local form of all, Attic, has common characteristics with Ionic, but it does not properly form a part of the Ionic dialect or of any other. The local forms of Elis, Locris, and Phocis are in many respects close to Doric ; but they are not properly

Doric. All the local forms of speech of a language thus cannot always be grouped into definite dialects.

Thus the notion of dialect is fleeting. It is the more so as it results from different historical conditions.

The Greek dialects result from the fact that there were successive and different thrusts of invaders over the Hellenic domain. The oldest wave which is observed is perhaps that of the Achaeans, whose history we do not have, but whom the recently discovered Hittite documents give an indication of about the thirteenth century B.C. and whose memory survives in legendary form in the Homeric poems ; there remain at a historical date the Arcadian dialects in the Peloponnese, Pamphylian in southern Asia Minor, and Cypriote, which to the very end marked an extreme limit of Hellenic expansion. The Ionian wave is doubtless approximately of the same period ; nothing remains of it in Greece proper ; but Euboea, the islands of the Aegean Sea, and the shores of the Mediterranean from the Black Sea to the coasts of Gaul have Ionian colonies. The most recent of these great thrusts is that of the Dorians which we can still perceive in progress at the beginning of the historical period of Greece and which covered many regions already entirely occupied by people speaking other Hellenic dialects, particularly a large part of the Peloponnese and Crete.

The dialects which are found in the Gallo-Romance domain have a completely different origin. All arise from the transformation of a substantially unitary language spoken in Gaul following the Roman conquest.

The dialects which resulted from this transformation have different aspects in Provence, Gascony, Normandy, and in île de France. We do not know very well either to what this diversity is due or why it happens that these regions have dialects which are similar to each other though distinct. As the boundaries of these linguistic regions often agree with old administrative boundaries, it has sometimes been supposed that the political divisions of a country condition the linguistic divisions. But if the country has been thus divided, it is in consequence of relations established among people; and if the administrative divisions of the Romans were maintained on the whole by the Christian church, it is because they responded in fact to natural needs. It is doubtless these relations which explain the dialectal similarities. There is coincidence, not cause.

It is necessary to consider another type of facts. In the modern world, and for a long time, there have been centers from which civilization has spread to a whole region. In France the provincial centers have only a secondary importance, and the influence of Paris has dominated since an early period. In Italy, on the other hand, there are several strong provincial centers. The economic and political importance of Venice has been of much value in the establishment of a Venetian dialect.

The existence of dialects has important consequences for the comparatist ; but these consequences differ according to the way in which the dialects have been established.

Sometimes the common language was one as much as a language can be. For the Romance languages this is the case for « Common Romance », which is the normal speech of a sole city, Rome. At the most one must consider, according to Gröber's hypothesis, the date when Latin was brought to the area where it spread : Sardinian had preserved the distinction between short i and long $\bar{e}$ and between short u and long $\bar{o}$ because at the time when Sardinia was conquered Rome still distinguished between $\breve{i}$ and $\bar{e}$ and between $\breve{u}$ and $\bar{o}$; Gallo-Romance (just as the majority of the Romance dialects) had a sole reflex of $\breve{i}$ and $\bar{e}$ and of $\breve{u}$ and $\bar{o}$ because at the time when the conquest took place and Latin was established, the tendency for $\breve{i}$ and $\bar{e}$ and for $\breve{u}$ and $\bar{o}$ to merge already existed. But, in sum, the origin of the Romance languages is a single language.

It is a different matter for Common Indo-European. Several differences which are observed among the Indo-European languages are found simultaneously in languages near to each other, so that we are led to posit that the point of departure for these differences is found in differences already existing in Indo-European.

Take, for example, the numeral « ten » : Greek *déka*, Latin *decem*, on the one hand, and Sanskrit *dáśa*, Armenian *tasn*, on the other. The Germanic and Celtic forms rest on forms having a medial k ; the Iranian, Slavic, and Baltic forms rest on forms having medially a kind of sibilant. From this point

of view, there are thus two groups of Indo-European
dialects. The same dialects have for the interrogative-
indefinite in Greek, Latin, Celtic, and Germanic a *qu*
or the reflexes of a *qu*, as Latin *quis*, and in Indo-
Iranian, Slavic, Baltic, and Armenian a *k* or the
reflex of a *k*, as Sanskrit *káḥ* « who », Lithuanian
kas, etc. This would tend to indicate that there were
two dialectal groups in Indo-European, one represented by Greek, Italo-Celtic, and Germanic, the other
by Slavic, Baltic, Armenian, and Indo-Iranian. From
the point of view of the velar consonants, this distribution would be exact, and we speak often of a group
of *satəm* languages (from an Iranian form of the
numeral « hundred ») and a group of *centum* languages (from the Latin form) for Indo-European.

But if we examine other facts, we find other distri-
butions. Thus the distinction between *o* and *a* is
preserved in Armenian, Greek, and Italo-Celtic ; but
it is obliterated in Germanic, Baltic, Slavic, and Indo-
Iranian. This time, Germanic goes with Slavic, etc.,
and Armenian with Greek, etc.

Thus we do not succeed in positing definite
dialects within Indo-European but differences of
treatment for certain phonological, morphological,
and lexical facts. And each of these differences has
its own boundaries. Thus the domain of Common
Indo-European was crossed by lines marking the areas
where different forms were used from several points
of view. And these lines, called isoglosses, agree only
partially with each other.

This state of things agrees with that which is observed in many cases. Thus the Gallo-Romance domain and the Lithuanian domain are crossed by some isoglosses which do not agree with others marking the boundaries of other linguistic features.

This coincidence between types of facts now observable and those which we are led to attribute to Indo-European shows how real the picture is which comparison gives of Indo-European. It is not a matter of a mere scheme but of an object as variable as reality itself.

Many changes which differ in each area arise after the period of unity, as a result of innovations which have occurred. Here is a typical example. Celtic inherited an old q^w like that preserved in Lat. *quis*. It shows, however, a tendency which appears in every part of the group where this sound is preserved : k^w tends to go to p and g^w to b. The passage of g^w to b was accomplished easily because Celtic already possessed a b which attracted the old g^w. But, by a singular peculiarity, Celtic had lost Indo-European p ; consequently, in going to p, q^w would have had to give rise to a p which no longer existed in the language ; this was sufficient to prevent q^w from going to p in the Irish group, and it is for this reason that **eqwos* « horse » became Irish **eq(os)*, whence *ech*. In Gaulish and Brittonic, on the other hand, the tendency of q^w towards p was stronger, and q^w went to p, so that the word **eqwos* became *epos* in Gaulish (and a similar form in Brittonic). The dialectal division was produced by virtue of events which are possibly later than the Common Celtic period. Once produced, it is responsible for subsequent differences ; for the two words consequently show profound differences and have necessarily different histories.

We see that the notion of dialect is somewhat hazy in all respects. Thus the comparatist cannot be content with it ; he is obliged to seek a field of observation more exactly delimited.

VI.

LINGUISTIC GEOGRAPHY

Ever since we have been applying ourselves to positing precise and regular correspondences between the phonological and morphological facts of a « common language » and the later attested languages, we have sought pure and unitary linguistic types where the rules might be applied with rigor. The great languages include elements too diverse. Already by definition dialects do not have unity. It was thought that the popular dialect observed in a locality of small extent would furnish this elementary unity which the linguist needs. And local dialects were studied.

Monographs have been written on very diverse dialects, some short and superficial, others detailed and in depth. The precise monographs contain important data for whoever wishes a fundamental understanding of one type of languages. They are highly instructive for general linguistics. But for the comparatist who wishes to reconstruct the history of a linguistic group, monographs on local dialects are not sufficient and are difficult to use.

In a domain of moderate extent as the Gallo-Romance domain, there are more than thirty thousand localities whose dialect it would be necessary to describe. The task clearly exceeds the personnel and material resources which linguists have at their disposal. Supposing that it could be accomplished, the linguist would be overwhelmed by a mass of data which he would not be able to handle. There would be, moreover, infinite repetitions : although each locality has its own peculiarities, the same facts and types of facts are found over broad domains.

Another difficulty : data gathered by different observers are not exactly comparable to each other. If the investigation has not been organized and conducted according to the same rules for the whole area studied, each monograph is presented in a different way, and the facts which are found in one cannot be compared immediately with those of another. Even in the favorable — and rare — case where the investigation has been organized and the monographs are made on a sole model, the observers have neither been able to observe nor to write down things in precisely the same way. It is, furthermore, inevitable that investigators are found for certain areas more than for others. And the density of the observations is not comparable.

Finally, dialects do not have the unity which has been attributed to them a priori. Persons of the same village, even if it is small, often have different ways of speaking according to their age, social position, occupations, etc. Not all the informants are natives ; not all are equally faithful to local usage. If a monograph of a local dialect takes account of these individual differences, it becomes complicated, and it is difficult to make use of it for comparison. If it neglects them, it does not give a correct idea of the state of the dialect ; it arbitrarily simplifies ; it schematizes rather than describes.

When we desire to proceed to the study of a group of modern dialects by comparative means, the investigation should be organized in such a way that it can immediately serve for comparison.

It is necessary at the outset to have observations distributed in an almost equal manner in the whole of the domain studied. The ideal would be to observe all localities. But in a normal domain where similar dialects are found in an area of some extent, and the dialect of each locality does not differ essentially from that of the neighboring locality, it is sufficient to examine localities picked at random so that we may have a system of observations comprising the whole country and furnishing specimens of all types. The tighter the network is, the less risk we run of letting important particulars escape and the surer we are of tracing exact boundaries for each fact. But the essential thing for the comparatist is to possess data which permit him to appraise the whole domain in the same way.

In the second place, it is necessary that the data be comparable to each other and that the information

which is gathered concern facts of the same order :
the same words, so that we may have the forms taken
by one word of the common language in the whole
domain, or words of the same meaning, the same
forms, or grammatical forms of the same value, etc.

To answer this double need, it is necessary to pre-
pare a questionnaire which is completed in all the
localities where the investigation is to be made. The
way in which given sentences are said in each of
the investigated localities is noted. This procedure
for the questionnaire has grave inconveniences : the
language in which the question is posed — which is
in principle the general language of the country —
runs the risk of influencing the local informant and
of diverting him from his own dialect. To have one
response and one alone for each locality, we have to
interrogate a sole informant ; and since the local
dialect is not unitary, this informant is more or less
unsuited for representing the whole dialect. The
procedure is rough and approximate. But it is the
only one possible.

We can consider two ways of conducting the investigation. Either we take a questionnaire which is
completed on the spot by a person as qualified as
possible to indicate the way in which things are said
in the dialect : this has been the procedure in
Germany. Or we send an investigator who interrogates
one person in each place examined and notes his
response ; this was done for the atlas of Gallo-
Romance dialects. Provided with a questionnaire pre-

pared by Gilliéron, Edmont alone visited all the
localities which were to be examined, chose a sole
informant in each, and noted the way in which this
informant rendered the sentences of the questionnaire.
The advantage of this second procedure is that it
presents pieces of evidence which are rigorously
comparable to each other and that we do not have
to take account of the distortions which result from
the personality of different investigators. This advantage is so great that the same technique has been
employed for investigations made later, and, for
example, a sole observer, Scheuermeier, is conducting
the whole investigation for the atlas of the Romance
dialects (other than the dialects of the French type)
of Switzerland and the northern Italian dialects which
Jaberg and Jud have organized.

At first sight the results obtained by such summary
procedures might appear suspect. But observations
made concerning points not very distant from each
other are mutually controlled, and verification
results from comparison itself. Moreover, the procedure of the investigation does not exclude that of
the monograph ; and it is sufficient to compare the
results of the investigation with monographs already
made or with new research to appraise the value of
the observations gathered by the investigator. Concerning the atlas of the Gallo-Romance dialects executed
by Gilliéron with the observations which Edmont had
gathered, there have been numerous verifications : in
several areas it was followed by detailed investigations

bearing on all the dialects of a limited area, like those of Millardet for the Landes, Bruneau for the Ardennes, and Oscar Bloch for the Vosges ; these minute investigations have in general confirmed essentially the correctness of Edmont's observations. We can point out errors of detail ; but nowhere do these slight errors vitiate the investigation in any fundamental way.

The results obtained have been important, and such that we have begun to increase investigations of this kind. In France an atlas for Corsica has been made, and another is appearing for the Breton dialects of French Armorica. A Catalan atlas is on the way to publication. We have already mentioned the atlas which Jaberg, Jud, and Scheuermeier are preparing. A young Frenchman, Tesnière, is now publishing a detailed study on the forms of the dual in Slovene based on an investigation of the geographical type.

The sole fact that the results of the investigation lend themselves to being indicated on maps, each devoted to a given fact, facilitates the work. We know that statistics gain in clarity by being expressed graphically. The linguist who sees on a single map or on two or three maps which he can juxtapose the facts relating to a problem has the essential elements for the solution under his eyes at one glance.

Already research on Gallo-Romance has been renewed by the *Atlas* of Gilliéron and Edmont. The studies evoked by the publication of the *Atlas* are increasing, and other studies where consideration is taken above all of data gathered in a whole area are continually appearing.

For comparison has found in these investigations an instrument of work superior to everything which it possessed and precisely adapted to its needs. For the first time we had clearly presented a set of data immediately comparable to each other and distributed throughout the whole domain studied. Whoever has written works of comparative grammar knows how we suffer from the fact that the facts compared present differences of level which we must disregard : the comparatist who works on the Indo-European languages makes use of data whose dates stretch over a space of some three thousand years, which abound at certain moments and are completely lacking at others, which exist for one area while all information is lacking for another. Before making a comparison, it is necessary to criticize in detail all the elements. In the comparitive grammar of the Indo-European languages there are few comparisons which are not weak on some side.

Already the results obtained by the geographical method are striking.

The problem of « dialect » has found its solution. We had often asked ourselves how to trace the boundaries between dialects. On the one hand, the dialect appeared as a set showing particular characteristics and in opposition to other dialects. On the other hand, we did not succeed in finding precise boundaries for dialects. Formerly, one observer who

departed from Bordeaux to determine the boundary
between the northern and southern Gallo-Romance
dialects had to give up marking a frontier and had
stopped without finishing his work. Yet it was sufficient to compare maps to perceive the truth.

Each linguistic fact has its proper boundaries.

But in certain areas we find a bundle of boundaries
of specific facts, boundaries which are sometimes
parallel and sometimes cross each other. There is no
boundary between the northern and southern Gallo-
Romance dialects ; there is a bundle of boundaries
of specific facts, many of which are near to each
other. To the north and south of this bundle, the
dialects have numerous features in common. The
opposition between the north and south is clear ; but
it cannot be marked by a single line.

In a characteristic way this bundle follows approximately the route which the railroad which goes from
Bordeaux to Lyon still follows, that is, it makes a
pronounced point to the north, to pass by the foot
of the Massif Central on the north side. The whole
Massif Central thus belongs to the type of southern
dialects. The influences which have given the dialects
of the northern part of France their special aspect,
so far from the Latin type, have stopped before the
mountainous Massif which occupies the center of
France. It is not the Loire which is a boundary ; it
is a group of high places, which are, in fact, hard to
cross and which roads necessarily skirt. The northern
French type goes much further south both in the west,

where it reaches Bordeaux, and in the east, where it
goes to the south of Lyon. Here the border of the
dialects is explained by a geographical fact, which
has conditioned historical events.

In the second place, owing to the great multitude
of facts observed, the intermediate period between
the common language and the later languages becomes
clear. It is the name for « bee » which Gilliéron
chose to illustrate the results of the geographical
method in a particularly profound way. It was known
by consideration of rules of phonological correspondence that the French word *abeille* cannot be native
to northern France and is borrowed from southern
dialects. But this brute fact would not reveal the
history of the word *abeille* in French. It was sufficient to examine a map where the names for « bee »
are shown to perceive that these names vary with the
regions of northern France : in one place, *abeille*, a
term which has come from the south ; in another,
mouche à miel ; in another, *mouchette ;* in another,
avette. This variety, for an insect used everywhere
since the Roman period, shows that the old name has
disappeared ; and the maps reveal an eliminated
name in some places : it is *é,* the form which Latin
apem normally took in northern France. Because it
was too short, this name was eliminated nearly
everywhere, to be replaced by new names which show
the difficulty in which the speakers found themselves.
In the word *mouchette,* Gilliéron finds by a bold
hypothesis, which has been contested but is particu-

larly attractive, an adaptation of a compound *mouche-é(p)* to which one would have recourse to get out of the difficulty caused by the rather great reduction of *apem* in northern France ; such a compound, moreover, could also have existed only virtually, and *mouchette* could have been substituted for it immediately ; for at the moment when phonological or morphological changes of this kind take place, innovations tend to be regulated immediately according to the existing system and to take their place among forms already established. The south, which had *apicula*, extended already in the Roman period, just as *ouis* was extended to *ouicula* (Fr. *ouaille*), did not have such a difficulty and furnished *abeille* to the Parisian area. For the schematic information which we had before on the origin of Fr. *abeille* is substituted a complex history where the reality is apparent.

Taking inspiration from these results, we shall better interpret the facts even when we have at our disposal meager and less easily comparable data. Very often it is sufficient to arrange facts geographically to understand their history.

Take, for example, the idea of « to grind, mill (grain) » in Indo-European. There is a present of the type **meləmi* or **moləmi* « I grind » which is indirectly preserved in Slavic, Baltic, Germanic, Celtic, and Italic and whose old form we have been able to reconstruct above (cf. p. 43). This verb is not found either in Indo-Iranian, Armenian, or Greek : this is not an accident and is not because the peoples who spoke

these languages were ignorant of grinding. For names
of cereals justly figure in these languages : we have
(except in Indo-Iranian) the root meaning « to till ».
But it is because there is another root meaning « to
grind » : *aléō* « I grind » in Greek, *alam* in Armenian, and this root has also left clear traces in Indo-
Iranian. We thus see that the idea of « to grind
(grain) » is expressed in different ways in two continuous domains of Indo-European.

The root **melə-*, which means « to grind, mill
(grain) » from Slavic to Italic, is not unknown to the
other languages ; but it is found there in the more
general sense of « to crush, to pound », as in Sanskrit
mṛnắti « he crushes », Armenian *malem* « I pound »
or in popular Greek verbs like *mullō* or the form
with reduplication *moimullō*, which is found in the
popular Ionian authors. And the agreement between
the root **melə-* and that of Greek *aleō* results from
the fact that just as Latin has *mola* « millstone »
beside *molo* « I grind », Greek, which has lost the
noun for the old millstone (preserved from India to
the Celtic world), has formed *mulē* « millstone »
from the root meaning « to crush ». The geographical
distribution of words gives an indication of a complete
history in spite of the poverty of the data.

From comparison of maps often results the explanation of surprising facts. Thus there is in southern
France an area where the expected reflex of the word
for « rooster », *gallu(m)*, has disappeared. In this
small area « rooster » is designated by strange names

which betray a difficulty in which the language found itself : « rooster » is called, for example, « pheasant » or « vicar ». But if we compare other maps, we see that in this area -*tt*- corresponds to Latin -*ll*- : the word **gat* for « rooster » was consequently merged with the word *gat* for « cat », old **gattu(m)*, which also became Italian *gatto*. It would be awkward to designate « cat » and « rooster » by the same name : the name for « rooster » has disappeared. And the language has got out of the difficulty by obvious artifices. When a notion is indicated by such peculiar methods, in general it is because an old name, excluded for one reason or another (the causes are diverse), has had to be replaced : the imagination of speakers is given free rein in such cases.

Everywhere that we have been able to apply the geographical method it has given rise to decisive progress. It requires investigations as extensive as possible and the utilization of all the data which we possess about a whole linguistic domain. The comparative method gains thereby a precision, an extent, and an ease hitherto unforeseen.

And this is, however, what we should expect : comparative grammar which works with systems of correspondences gains less by considering dialects — which are not of interest to it in themselves — than facts of the same order in the set of dialects which continue the same « common language ».

It is needless to recall, as we have already observed on p. 43, that since every dialect has its own system,

it is always necessary to consider the place of each
fact of detail in each of these systems. An examination exclusively of words and forms furnished by
investigations and noted geographically would run the
risk of causing one word or a small group of words,
one form or a small group of forms to be studied in
an isolated way. Such atomistic effort would completely ruin any historical linguistics. Linguistic geogra-
phy has had the merit of placing in full evidence the
singularity of the history of each word and of each
form. But this singularity has its place in systematic
wholes, and anyone who considered isolated facts
without representing them in these systems would run
the risk of committing errors even worse than those
committed by the linguist who exclusively considers
systems and does not study with a very sure critique
each of the special facts from which these systems
are made.

VII.

MIXED LANGUAGES

For a long time historical linguistics has operated with the tacitly accepted hypothesis that language is transmitted from generation to generation, each child reproducing to the best of his ability the speech of his environment. Such is the case which seems normal and which we often observe in fact.

But it happens that a people changes its language. This is not an exceptional fact : among countries whose history is known — and we know that in the most favorable case history established by means of texts does not anywhere go back beyond about five thousand years, a short period in relation to the total development of humanity — there is scarcely a people which has not changed its language at least once, and generally more than once.

Of all countries, Egypt is that whose history goes back farthest and where there is the most preservation ; after having lasted during about four thousand years of the historical period, Egyptian went out of use and was replaced by Arabic, even though the basis of the population did not appreciably change ;

the Macedonian conquest brought a Greek colony, especially to Alexandria, and produced the Hellenization of small groups of rulers ; but the basis of the population remained the same, even taking account of the emigrants from Syria. On the territory of what is now France, Gaulish must have arrived with the Celtic conquest during the first half of the millennium which preceded the Christian era ; then it gave way to Latin after the Roman conquest ; the Gaulish conquest does not appear to have changed the population, and the Roman conquest certainly brought only few new elements. It would be easy to multiply examples : changes of language often occur. It is important to examine under what conditions these changes are made and what their effects are.

The easiest case to observe is that which is presently found nearly everywhere in Europe. In each area there is a group of local dialects of the same family and a written language, a language of civilization, which serves for all general uses and for relations with the whole country, and is the language of the government, school, administration, press, etc. In such cases the written language has a strong influence on the local dialects.

Then two movements of different directions take place, which lead to the same final result.

The local dialect is filled with elements borrowed from the general language, which alone is in a position to respond to the new needs of civilization and whose prestige is great in relation to the local dialect : it is the language of the most powerful and most cultivated people. In studying the local dialects of Roman Gaul, Gilliéron has found that in the cases where they encountered difficulty, these dialects sought in general French the means for getting out of the difficulty. Thus, far from furnishing a pure tradition resulting from their own history, the Gallo-Romance dialects contain to a great extent general French elements « spoken in patois ». Studies on the Gallo-Romance dialects now contain an important chapter on the processes by which these dialects adapted French words. As French and the dialect belong to the same family, they have regular correspondences for the old stock of their vocabulary, and it is not difficult for persons using the local dialect to make patois forms with French words or to bring into the patois French expressions by taking account of these correspondences. However, this work of uneducated persons is often so well done that the linguist has difficulty in distinguishing what is really native in the patois from what is adapted.

The superiority of the general language both for its value and for the means which it gives to communicate with other people is such that in spite of old usages, one soon tends to prefer this general language to the local dialect, as one substitutes urban custom for local customs. But it is less easy to change language than custom. If the local dialects of France are often in large part French « spoken in patois », the French used in the village is often patois « spoken

in French ». In many cases it is sufficient to change
the local word a little to make a correct French word
from it : the village word *lwé* becomes French as
soon as it is pronounced *lwa (loi)*. The Berrichon
word *lavwé* is a little more difficult to frenchify ; it
is not enough to pronounce it *lavwa ;* it is necessary
to add *r* (Fr. *lavoir)* ; there is thus a chance that
lavwé may survive for a while ; but everyone ends
up saying *lavoir* in the French way. What survive
longest are certain grammatical usages fixed in the
memory, of which one is hardly aware, as was indicated above on p. 40. These usages are eliminated in
turn and thus, bit by bit, the local dialect is replaced
by general French. This movement now takes place
in a rapid way, more quickly in certain areas than in
others : general French is eliminating the local
dialect in central France more than in Picardy, for
example. But the movement takes place everywhere,
and we already perceive the moment when all study
of local dialects in northern France will have become
impossible because these dialects will have gone out
of use. They were still usual everywhere in the
villages at the end of the eighteenth century ; and
even in the first part of the nineteenth century the
manner of speaking in all the villages of France
preserved at least considerable remains of the local
type.

The French situation is not a novelty in history. In
the fifth century B.C. nearly every Greek locality
had its own dialect. Beginning with this period, the

stronger and stronger action of the general language eliminated the local peculiarities one after the other, and a common language, based on Attic usage, spread to all of Greece. In spite of many reactions, this language imposed itself everywhere, and we see that its use had become more or less universal in the Hellenic domain from the imperial period. The modern Greek dialects, which have once again diverged from each other, all continue this common language. And we hardly perceive anywhere any slight survival of the local Greek dialects which existed prior to the generalization of the common language.

But this generalization does not take place without reactions which modify the general language. The Greek which was generalized is not pure Attic. The features which spread everywhere are above all those which were common to Attic and Ionic, and some peculiarities proper to Attic besides. But other peculiarities quite special to Attic were not accepted. For example, ss was preferred to the pronunciation tt of the corresponding Attic forms, and *melissa* « bee » was used as in Ionic and in the majority of the dialects, not *melitta*, which was the form of Athens. As Athens also conformed with time to common usage, Attic peculiarities disappeared. Thus « no one » came to be expressed by *outhēs* in Athens by the fourth century B.C. ; this Attic form did not prevail, and the old form *oudēs*, which had survived outside of Athens, finally returned to Athens. Modern Greek consequently has *den*, which is the ancient neuter *oudén* « nothing », to express « not ». Common Greek thus does not continue purely a sole dialect ; it contains elements belonging to dialects near to each other, but distinct.

Even general French, which is the language of Paris, is undergoing provincial influences in spite of the purism which prevails in France.

Thus a general language is more or less a mixed language by reason of the way in which it is established and the complexity of the elements which enter into it.

This can go far. General Italian is based on Tuscan usage ; but the pronunciation does not admit Tuscan peculiarities, and it is usually taught that general Italian is a *lingua toscana in bocca romana* (« Tuscan language in a Roman mouth »). General English rests on the usage of London ; but situated at the meeting point of various dialects, London has in its dialect features which come from different areas. Thus general languages, because of the fact that they are established to respond to the needs of people whose origins are different, do not rest on only one tradition, even in the most favorable cases.

There can even be artifice in the way in which general languages are established. Thus the grammarian Vuk, who gave written Serbo-Croatian its form, based himself on the dialect of a Serbo-Croatic region where the old *x (h)* was lost ; and he had begun by establishing the language without *h*. After reflection it seemed better to him to take account of the dialects of a more archaic type where *h* was preserved. The language which he established was thus composite. And as individuals belonging to areas where *h* had disappeared had difficulty in pronouncing *h*, there is fluctuation and much trouble in general Serbo-Croatian usage on this point.

The extension of a general language is not limited to cases where the local dialects belong to the same linguistic type and have the same origin as this general language. When the general language is clearly distinct from the local dialects, the facts present themselves in a way different from the case studied ; but the development is similar in several respects.

On the one hand, the native language on which a different general language is superimposed is reduced to local and inferior usages. Consequently, it is filled with elements borrowed from the general language. It is for this reason that in French Armorica Breton is filled with French words and expressions. It can be spoken with carelessness and lose some of its most characteristic features. For example, the Breton of the region of Vannes has very much deteriorated. A language reduced to local usages tends to lose a larger and larger part of its elements. In general, this has little importance for the history of the language ; for a language so degraded ends up disappearing completely.

The usage of the general language, which is more convenient and classes the speaker among cultivated people, spreads more and more. But the people who thus pass to the general language cannot speak it exactly as those for whom it is traditional. In addition to local terms designating animals, plants, customs, and regional forms for which the general language does not have words so precise, there survive among individuals who have passed to a new language old ways of expressing themselves ; the pronunciation is not ordinarily reproduced in a perfect way.

Consider, for example, what is happening in France. Although the northern and southern dialects are both Gallo-Romance, they differ to an extent that a person is not completely understood in every region if he uses a local dialect. When the southerners use general French, which is often today the only language which the inhabitants of cities know, they pronounce it in a special way which is different in each region. The characteristics of the vowels are greater in southern than in northern France ; the vocalic timbres used are different ; the nasal vowels are differently articulated ; the mute e's, whose distribution in French is a delicate and subtle thing, are placed in an incorrect way ; in brief, the whole pronunciation is different. The grammar even contains differences : the simple preterite, whose use the written language has maintained, but which no longer exists in spoken French of the region of Paris, is frequent among southerners speaking French. Thus even in a case where, as in French, there is a sole type of language instruction, a powerful purist influence, and a usage established with a rigor nowhere exceeded and rarely equalled, the generalization of the language does not take place without a strong adaptation to local customs. In being generalized, French is dissolved into regional French dialects, and the model of Paris is not exactly reproduced in any province. If these regional French dialects have never been described with precision, they nonetheless exist. The influence of the « local substratum » makes itself felt, so to speak, and to the extent that we can observe the spread of general languages, this influence appears inevitable.

Doubtless the action of school and of the written language and the desire which individuals have of speaking correctly tend to unify the form of the general language ; but this unification cannot be perfect. The norm of the language may be the same everywhere ; but it is not realized in the same way everywhere.

Doubtless there is even something more profound : experiments indicate that though acquired anatomical characteristics are not transmitted, there may be an inheritance of acquired habits. Linguistic usage has to the highest degree the character of a set of acquired habits. In learning a new language, individuals do not lose their heredity. Tendencies which are present in the native language today can consequently also be manifested in the newly adopted language. We thus understand how Latin may have undergone particularly profound transformations in domains where it replaced other languages with completely different tendencies, notably Gaulish. We know, for example, that one of the features which characterize Celtic is a strong tendency to change, to conform to the neighboring vowels, and even to eliminate consonants between vowels. Nowhere in the Gallo-Romance domain, especially in French, have the Latin intervocalic consonants been more altered, or even eliminated, than they have in French : *lepore(m)* becomes *lièvre*, and *amatam* becomes *aimée*. We are thus led to suppose that the most characteristic innovations of French would be due not only to the way in which Latin was pronounced in Gaul, but to an inheritance of acquired habits by individuals speaking Gaulish. With this form of hypothesis, the objections which are often made to the substratum theory are immediately resolved. The passage of closed u to $ü$ in the Gallo-Romance domain and in Alsace would not be an immediate survival of Gaulish, but the distant effect of certain acquired habits transmitted by heredity.

If the explanation — at least partial — of the diversity of the forms taken in different domains by a generalized language is often contested, it is because the facts are considered in too mechanical a way : we must not expect to find in the generalized language peculiarities of the « substratum » in crude form. The action is complex and is manifested in forms which are not very apparent at first sight.

Granting this, a generalized language is a more or less mixed language in the domains where it extends, since beside a universal norm we observe the influence

— doubtless profound — of local usages and of local habits.

Moreover, and even apart from these interior influences, borrowing is sufficient to give a language a new aspect if it becomes frequent. The fact that English owes to Latin and French more than half of its vocabulary is sufficient in itself to differentiate it from the other Germanic languages. Even its pronunciation is affected, since the borrowed words have preserved their accentuation, and the Germanic accentuation on the initial syllable of the word has consequently ceased to preserve its character of constancy. Expressions can be borrowed : the German expression *was für* can be transposed to a Slavic expression *čto za*. There even arise expressions whose elements are taken from two languages : in Latin, Greek *kath-ena* (literally « by one ») was in part calqued, in part borrowed, and the result is **cata-uno*, **cat-uno*, whence Spanish *cadauno*, Italian *caduno* « each ».

Whoever speaks of « borrowing » admits that the speaker is aware of two distinct languages. And, in fact, in languages with complicated morphology like the Indo-European languages, the Semitic languages, the Bantu languages, or even in languages with simpler morphology but with well defined characteristics of grammatical categories, the speaker must always speak a certain language ; he is aware of speaking either one language or another ; and he cannot mix the morphology of one language with that of another.

As degenerate as his Breton may be, the inhabitant of the region of Vannes knows whether he is speaking French or Breton. For he uses two essentially distinct morphologies according to the situation. Marr has supposed that Armenian morphology, whose Indo-European character is manifest, included elements due to a population which existed prior to the arrival in the Armenian land of people speaking an Indo-European language ; but he has not succeeded in proving this hypothesis and has not convinced any of the linguists outside of his own school who are interested in the history of Armenian.

For languages like those of the Far East which have a minimum of morphology, and in which the sentence is made with the help of definite word order and with accessory words, we can better understand that the speaker borrows processes from two languages. We can easily conceive that an Annamese may mix some features of Chinese with his own dialect. The juxtaposition of two languages of this sort is relatively easy. And perhaps it is not an accident that it is difficult to recognize and establish language families in the Far East.

In fact, up to now cases have not been found where one has been led to posit that the morphological system of a given language results from a mixture of the morphologies of two distinct languages. In all the cases observed up to the present time, there is one continuous tradition for a language ; there can be a more or less large number of borrowings, and these borrowings can occasion certain new processes of word formation ; the tradition can be of the normal type : transmission of the language from the old to the young, or result from a change of language : learning of a language of communication by a people which finally abandons its own language. But there is only one tradition for the morphological system.

Nevertheless, we cannot affirm that in certain favorable cases there have not been any real « mixtures ». But if one should happen to find them, the task of the linguist would be difficult. If we have been able to succeed in reconstructing the history of some languages by comparison, it is because we were sure that each new system had to be explained as coming from a single system. In the case where one would have to take account of two initial systems and of their reactions on each other, the present methods would not be sufficient. For the right that one would have of choosing between two series of original forms would cause such an arbitrariness that every proof would become almost unrealizable. In spite of the hypotheses made in this direction, linguists have, fortunately, never yet been surely in the face of such a difficulty. If the difficulty really happens to occur, linguistics will have to work out new methods more delicate than those which are described here in order to overcome it, and it would remain to test them.

VIII.

GENERAL FORMULAS OF CHANGE

Both to respond to its function which is to serve as
a means of communication among members of a
society and because the normal tendency of every
social group is to establish an exact conformity
among its members, there tends to be only one language for each social group. The manner of pronunciation and the morphology which individuals who
speak the same language use agree in many respects
with rigorous precision. Details of forms and nuances
of meaning which the most precise grammarian has
difficulty in discerning and in formulating are often
maintained during successions of generations without
undergoing any notable alteration. These minute
agreements do not exclude strong divergences affecting
some points ; but these partial divergences are only
possible precisely because language has a foundation
of unity and speakers of the same group feel that
they belong to the same type.

When changes are produced, they must consequently
affect the group in its entirety, or risk effecting its
dislocation. And it is, in fact, established that lin-

guistic changes affect all the speakers. Language
lives only by virtue of society ; if individuals set
about modifying language in an independent way, it
would no longer respond to its object. Thus, like
preservations of old usages, innovations are general.
We do not yet have certain data concerning the way
in which this generality is established. We perceive
at least that innovations are in part general and in
part generalized. They depend on conditions common
to all individuals, but their establishment is doubtless
due much to the feeling which individuals have of
having to use the same linguistic type. Society often
reacts in a strong way against individual innovations
in language.

What shows that change is not due to the more or
less fortuitous generalization of individual innovations
is that parallel changes take place in cases whose
similarity the linguist sees, but in which the speaker
can perceive only differences. The Romance languages
offer a significant example in this regard. The old
long $\bar{o}$ and short $\breve{u}$ of Latin became a closed o as the
old form of the majority of the Romance dialects ;
thus the accented vowel of *nōdum* and that of *gulam*
become the same vowel *eu* in French *nœud* and *gueule*
(the difference of orthography is without significance,
and the slight differences which are observed are due
to the difference of position in French); the old long
$\bar{e}$ and short $\breve{\imath}$ also became closed e : Lat. *mē* became
moi and Lat. *bibit* became *boit* in French. The two
mergers are explained by common conditions, of

which the principal ones are the loss of quantitative
oppositions and the fact that in Latin long vowels
were closed and short vowels open : ō is related to
ŭ, as ē to ĭ. The relation of ō to ŭ is the same as that
of ē to ĭ ; but this theoretical fact is not visible to the
native speaker. The parallelism of innovations can
result only from the common effect of parallel
conditions.

If innovations are thus both common to different
individuals, without there being action between them,
and parallel to each other, it is because to a certain
degree they depend on general conditions.

All linguists who have had to examine phonological
changes and to establish rules of correspondences
between different languages have felt that these
changes take place according to certain general types.
Some types of facts are observed in a large number
of cases. For example, the velar stops — really
characterized by the contact of the surface of the
tongue and the palate — are subject to palatalization
before prepalatal elements such as y, the vowels i, e,
and even the vowel a oriented towards e ; this is what
is observed in noting that in such cases k, g become
k', g' : the k of Fr. qui is completely different from
that of Fr. cou. These prepalatal k', g' are subject to
become tš, dž (č, ǰ) or ts (c), dz ; and these tš, dž
and ts, dz are subject to become simply š, ž and s, z.
For example, Lat. cinere(m) became Fr. cendre and
Lat. carbōne(m) became Fr. charbon. Such develop-

ments are observed almost everywhere in the world and in the most varied language families.

But there are more delicate formulas whose existence Grammont recognized in his fundamental work on consonantal dissimilation. If an articulatory movement is to be repeated in the same set of emissions of sound, the speaker tends to avoid this repetition.

This tendency does not affect all speech sounds alike ; there are articulatory movements which are less easy and general than others, and it is these which one avoids making twice in a brief interval. The assumption of special positions which the tongue must occupy for *l* and *r* and the lowering of the soft palate which is essential for *n* and *m* are movements whose repetition is often avoided.

Then suppression takes place in a definite order. For example if the old *uenēnu(m)* becomes Italian *veleno*, that is, if of the two *n*'s which the word contains, one has lost the lowering of the soft palate and in consequence has become *l*, it is the first *n* which is thus altered ; barring reaction due to special circumstances, of two *n*'s so placed, it is the first, not the second, which loses its nasalization. Thus there are general conditions which control the way in which dissimilation is produced, and these conditions can be formulated. Grammont has succeeded in determining them completely.

This permits us to recognize in many cases the way in which an innovation has taken place. We know, for example, that in the languages where the accent serves as the center of the word, the vowels of accented syllables are treated differently from the vowels of unaccented syllables. Two distinct types of alteration of unaccented vowels are observed here.

In certain languages the unaccented vowels tend to lose simultaneously a part of their duration and much of their characteristic timbre : they are often reduced to a more or less neutral timbre, as that of German *e* in unaccented syllables ; this *e* can, according to circumstances, rest on an old vowel of any timbre. We observe such alteration in Russian : the unaccented vowels are becoming more and more indistinct ; they have less and less a characteristic timbre, whereas the accented vowels are clearly pronounced.

In other languages, on the other hand, the unaccented vowels are altered in accordance with their degree of aperture : *e* and *o* become *i* and *u* ; and the vowels *i* and *u* are lost purely and simply ; this is what has happened in the modern northern Greek dialects.

In German, English, and Russian accented syllables are above all intense, and much more intense than unaccented syllables ; on the other hand, in modern Greek the vowels of accented syllables are characterized above all by their duration : they are longer than the others. If the unaccented vowels tend to lose their characteristic timbre, it is thus by virtue of the greater intensity of the accented vowels ; if the unaccented vowels tend to be closed, *e* and *o* into *i* and *u*, it is by virtue of the greater duration of the accented vowels : *i* and *u*, which are already by nature shorter vowels than *e* and *o*, can be shortened only by disappearing.

Consequently, where we observe facts comparable to those of the northern Greek type, there is reason to believe that this is by virtue of quantitative oppositions. For example, nothing permits us to attribute to the Armenian accent an intensity comparable to that of the modern English, German, or Russian accent : modern Armenian does not have a very intense accent ; thus if unaccented *i* and *u* were lost in old Armenian, whereas unaccented *a*, *e*, and *o* were maintained, it is doubtless because the accented vowels were apparently longer than the unaccented ones as in northern Greek. Likewise there is no reason to believe that initial Romance (called Vulgar Latin) had a very intense accent, and we know that the accent of modern French has a very weak intensity : thus it is arbitrary to suppose that at one moment of its history French had an accent of the German or Russian type ; it is not a weak accent of this type which produced the great reductions of vowels observed in the passage of Latin to French : if *camera* became *chambre*, it is not because *ca-* was accented with much more force than *me* and *ra*. The development is rather of the northern Greek type ; and, in fact, it affected the most open vowel, *a*, less than the other vowels : *nouu(m)* became *neuf*, whereas *noua(m)* became *neuve ;* the *u* of *nouu(m)* was lost from before the time of the first French texts, whereas the *a* of *noua(m)* was reduced to the so-called mute *e* ; and it is only in the course of the history of French, and even at a relatively recent date, that the *e* of *neuve* ceased to be pronounced.

The investigation of the general conditions under which phonological changes can take place is only at its beginning. But already we are finding many certain facts. For example, a consonant following another consonant is stronger, that is, more susceptible of lasting than a consonant placed between vowels ; the intervocalic *-t-* of *dōtāre* has disappeared in Fr. *douer ;* but the *-t-* preceded by *-k-* in *lactūca* has survived in Fr. *laitue.* There is in these facts something to guide the linguist.

However, exact formulas cannot yet be found in all cases. It is at least always necessary to observe the conditions proper to certain speech sounds. For example, *y*, far from entering into the rule for post-consonantal consonants, tends to be blended with the pronunciation of a preceding consonant so that it often loses its own existence while profoundly altering this consonant. But there could be written — Schleicher already attempted it, prematurely — a whole study on the combinations of *y* with preceding consonants and the manifold phenomena which result.

There are some complex cases : some groups of intervocalic consonants like *-mn-* admit of varied treatments. In Italian *-n-* is treated as if it were post-consonantal, and *somnu(m)* becomes *sonno ;* in French, on the other hand, *-mn-* forms a group which belongs entirely to the explosion, and it is *m* which dominates here, whence *somme* ; finally, in Spanish a complex speech sound is produced, and the result is *sueño*, where we do not properly find either *m* or *n*. It would not be worth while to attempt to reduce these treatments to a single formula. But it is not for all that impossible to posit formulas : the formulas do not apply to the whole development between an initial moment and different results more or less distant. The formulas of evolutionary general phonetics apply only at the moment when each partial change takes place. If *somnu(m)* became *sonno* in Italian, it is because at the moment when the assimilation took place, -*mn*- formed a group of two distinct consonants in which -*n*- was treated as post-consonantal. If *somnu(m)* became *somme* in French, it is because at the moment of the change -*mn*- was closely grouped and -*n*- had lost its autonomy. The conclusion follows that in a group such as -*mn*-, the nasal -*n*- is subject to lose its character of a post-consonantal consonant, something which is due to the special character of the nasals *m* and *n*.

Finally — and this is the essential feature — the formulas of evolutionary general phonetics indicate possibilities, not necessities. We can determine how a consonant placed between vowels is subject to change ; but this does not imply that it will change. A -*k*- placed between vowels is subject to change either into a velar spirant *x* (German *ch*) or into a voiced stop *g* ; and the *x* and *g* can later undergo other alterations due to their intervocalic position ; for example, the Romance *k* became *i* in French in a case such as *auca* becoming *oie* (now pronounced *wa*) ; but an Indo-European intervocalic *k* has survived everywhere in Slavic, and the *k* which is pronounced today in Polish *piekę* « I bake » has existed in this first person since Indo-European (the *i* of Fr. *cuis* represents the same element — after many successive transformations).

In morphology things happen in a less rigid way than in phonology. Morphology is the domain of survival.

A grammatical category which is explained by the mentality of people of a certain society persists long after this mentality has disappeared. People who see internal forces behind natural phenomena and events can classify ideas as animate and inanimate and distinguish systematically among the animate between what is male or likened to the male and what is female or likened to the female. We thus perceive how the tree which produces fruits can be feminine and the fruit neuter (inanimate gender) ; but such a mentality no longer existed in the Rome of the first century A.D., and an opposition as that between *pirus* « pear tree » (feminine) and *pirum* « pear » was no more than a survival. In modern French it would be very shocking to say *la ciel* or *le terre* ; but no one could say why, from the point of view of a Frenchman of today ; it is only by virtue of a secular tradition that the substantives are thus opposed.

A category which has had a strong meaning and a large use tends to lose its meaning and much of its function. The « subjunctive » was an essential part of the Latin verb, and the role of the subjunctive dominates Latin syntax. But the role of the subjunctive has continued to be restricted since the Common Romance period. Today in French the subjunctive serves as a substitute for forms lacking the imperative: besides *viens* (« come ! » singular), *venez* (« come ! » plural) we have *qu'il vienne* (« let him come ! »), *qu'ils viennent* (« let them come ! »). And there are some expressions where the subjunctive is still in force : *je veux qu'il vienne* (« I wish that he come »), *il faut qu'il vienne* (« it is necessary that he come »). But modern French no longer has the sense of the meaning of the subjunctive. Thus the popular language is restricting its usage more and more : literary French has *je doute qu'il vienne* (« I doubt that he may come »), but in everyday French, one tends to say : *je doute s'il viendra* (« I doubt whether he will come »). An expression like : *s'il fait cela et qu'il dise ce qu'il pense, il aura tort* (« if he does that and should say what he thinks, he will be wrong ») is now archaic.

With this reservation, morphology evolves according to general formulas like phonology. A fundamental fact of the evolution of the Indo-European languages will furnish an example of this.

In Common Indo-European the noun and the verb were both inflected forms. There was no one form of the noun, that of the nominative case, for example, from which the others would have been derivatives : a noun consisted of a set of case forms none of which governed the others ; in Latin there is not one word « wolf » but a set *lupus, lupe, lupum, lupī, lupō,* where none of these five forms serves to form the others any more than it serves to form the plural *lupī, lupīs, lupōrum, lupīs ;* there is not one noun for « man », but a set *homō, hominem, hominis, hominī, homine,* etc. Likewise, there is not one form for « to go » which governs the others, but *eō, īs, it* and *ībam, ībō, eam, īrem,* etc.

In the course of the development of the Indo-European languages the nominal forms have sooner or later, but everywhere, tended to reduce their inflection ; except for the old Indo-Iranian forms, no Indo-European language presents completely all the declensional forms. And with time declension has disappeared in a large number of languages, as in the Romance languages and in English and Persian : or else the form of the nominative case has assumed a dominant importance, as in Slavic, or has served as a point of departure for other forms as in Armenian. However, all these languages have preserved a verbal inflection, if not as rich as the Indo-European inflection, at least varied, complex, and provided with many forms. Comparison of the French verb, which is still so encumbered with different forms, with the French noun, which is invariable, is significant.

This is not an accident ; Common Semitic had a

nominal inflection with three cases distinguished by their endings ; the oldest Akkadian (Babylonian) and classical Arabic alone give an idea of it ; late Akkadian and modern Arabic have eliminated it ; on the other hand, the Semitic verb has everywhere, even in a language as evolved as Aramaic, a conjugation rich in forms. And, generally, we often observe this contrast between the absence of nominal inflection and the richness of the verbal inflection.

This is due to the nature of the noun and the verb. The noun indicates an idea of permanent nature : a thing, a person, or a quality ; the verb indicates a process, whether it is a matter of an action proper or of a state : « he eats, he is asleep », etc. For the very reason that it indicates a permanent notion, the noun has a sole form or at most a principal form from which the others are derived. On the other hand, the verb, which indicates a process, has personal forms and the expression of nuances which vary with languages, but can be numerous. The fact that the forms of the noun and verb obey divergent tendencies thus results from the nature of things.

Whether in phonology or in morphology, the general formulas of development are explained by conditions common to all people or at least to a whole type of civilization.

IX.

SPECIFIC INNOVATIONS

The conditions common to all people or to a whole
type of civilization have the effect of maintaining
unity. But there are also conditions proper to certain
groups of people, to certain times, and to certain
areas. The result of these special conditions is that
a language, unitary at a given moment, is differentiated with time into distinct dialects.

As long as characteristic new tendencies do not
occur, the linguistic system does not essentially change.
The modifications which are caused by general tendencies to change do not ordinarily produce the crea-
tion of new speech sounds. Thus when a speech sound
loses one of its elements by dissimilation, the language
does not keep the peculiar sound which would result
purely and simply from the dissimilation. If the first
of the two *n*'s in an old *veneno* loses the lowering of
the soft palate, the result is not a very weak stop
without nasalization as we might expect ; this sound,
whose articulation would be insufficiently marked, was
immediately replaced by a sound of similar type existing in the language, and we have *veleno* ; the denasal-

ized *n* had only a virtual existence. Once the change was effected, there was an *l* in one more word, but not one more type of sound in the language.

We frequently observe facts of this type. At a relatively recent date French lost palatalized *l* which was a frequent sound ; this was only a simplification of articulation, and no important fact occurred which could cause a notable variation of the articulatory system. The elimination of palatalized *l* did not have the consequence of creating a new sound either : palatalized *l* was simplified to *y*, that is, to a sound which was found in current use in *miel* and *pied, yeux* and *aïeux*, etc. After the innovation French had many more *y*'s than it had had previously ; but the phonological system was not modified.

The old **sw-* and **tw-* have the reflex *k'* (aspirated *k*) in Armenian. This suppressed some cases of the consonant *w* ; but the *k'* so produced is identical with the *k'* of different origin which existed in Armenian in words like *k'an* « than » or *lk'anem* « I leave ».

In morphology the simple play of analogy only causes the use of existent categories to be enlarged, without creating new ones. If *dites, faites* are replaced by *disez, faisez* in French, the language has nothing new ; for we say *lisez, taisez*, etc. If *héstēka* was made in Greek beside *héstamen*, with -*k*- after *éthēka, éthemen*, this was only to facilitate the formation of the perfect ; the use of a process which originally was found only in two or three forms was much enlarged ;

but neither a new process nor a new category was established.

Experience shows that new phonological and morphological processes are created. In all the Indo-European languages we observe innovations which have transformed the language by introducing sounds hitherto unused, new grammatical forms, and even new categories. Thus there are specific innovations which cannot be traced to any tendency of universal character.

Indo-European had voiceless stops articulated with force where the explosion was not followed by any breath, so that the vocalic vibrations of the vowels began immediately after the explosion : this is the type of the voiceless p, t, k as we find them in the Romance languages and in Baltic, Slavic, and Iranian, for example. There were voiced stops more weakly articulated and accompanied by vibrations of the larynx from the moment of implosion : such are the b, d, g of the same languages. In Armenian, Germanic, and even in Celtic (here less radically), these types were replaced by others : the articulation of p, t, k became weaker, and a puff of breath was inserted between the explosion and the beginning of the laryngeal vibrations which characterize vowels ; with regard to b, d, g, the laryngeal vibrations did not begin at the very moment of implosion so that b, d, g so pronounced are related to the voiceless type (in French b, d, g of this sort have the effect of poorly made p, t, k). Thus the system of articulation of stops changed com-

pletely. The new system was less stable than the old
one ; and whereas the languages which have remained
faithful to the Indo-European type still present the
Indo-European state especially at the beginning of
words or in a protected post-consonantal position,
there have been numerous innovations of detail which
have often disturbed the parallelism — thus Armenian and Celtic have lost old initial p. This great
change of articulatory type was probably produced
abruptly, when Indo-European spread to new
populations.

But there are other specific changes which take place
after the change of language, often a long time
afterward, and arise only little by little, doubtless by
virtue of acquired hereditary tendencies. Thus in the
Germanic languages the pronunciation of the vowel
of the following syllable is being prepared at the
moment when a vowel is uttered ; this had important
consequences. Each of the Indo-European vowels was
either clearly prepalatal or clearly postpalatal ; on
the other hand, Germanic, with its tendency to pre-
pare an i or y when an a or o is pronounced, for
example, created mixed vowels like French eu and $ü$.
These vowels are very different in each Germanic
language and in each Germanic dialect. Extreme com-
plications resulted from this, particularly in Old
English and in the Scandinavian dialects. These innovations took place to a great extent a little before the
historical period of these languages or even during
the historical period. But they had begun long before.

Here again there is a specific innovation of Germanic, and this innovation affects the whole vocalic system which it radically transforms.

Innovations belonging to the same tendency can be completed at quite different times. Thus the consonantal forms corresponding to the vowels *i* and *u*, that is, *y* and *w*, were eliminated in Greek. But while *y* was unknown in all the Greek dialects from a period long before the historical period, and when the Phoenician alphabet was borrowed, the sign for yod was used to designate solely the vowel *i*, on the other hand, *w* (which is called digamma in Greek) survived long into the historical period ; certain texts of many dialects still have all the old *w*'s ; others, which preserve initial *w*, have already lost intervocalic *w* ; some peculiarities of Attic show that before the historical period *w* existed there. The elimination of *w* thus took place only long after the elimination of *y*. Nevertheless, the two phenomena result from the same fundamental tendency ; the language owes to this change a notable part of the difference of appearance which is observed between Indo-European and Greek.

Sometimes the unity of the tendency is masked by special accidents. Thus in Romance the old *y* and *w* tended to take a more consonantal character at the beginning of a word than that which the consonants *i* and *u* had in Latin. The consonant *i* became *dž*, whence Fr. *j* ; thus from *iam* we have Italian *gia* and French *ja-* (in *ja-mais*). Consonantal *u* also became more consonantal ; but Latin already had the labiodental f ; the voiced correspondent, v, was lacking : the consonantal form of u succeeded in filling this empty slot in the phonological system. As f and v are stable consonants, these spirants have survived. The treatment of consonantal i thus ceased to be parallel to that of consonantal u. In the interior of a word between vowels Latin had lost consonantal i well before the historical period whereas consonantal u survived ; the interior consonantal u also passed to the spirant pronunciation, v.

In morphology there are likewise specific tendencies, and from them result simultaneously losses and innovations.

There are several Indo-European languages in which the distinction of grammatical genders has been lost. Doubtless this distinction has not corresponded to anything in the mentality of civilized men for centuries. But it survives in the Romance languages and in German, Slavic, etc. where, without semantic value, it holds an important place among grammatical processes. We do not see that it had more reason to disappear in Armenian — where the distinction between stems in -o- and -$\bar{o}$- is maintained in the declension of substantives — than in German, for example. Armenian has no trace of it. There is really a specific tendency here ; for in western Iranian, which is neighboring, the distinction of genders has also been abolished. And it is not fortuitous that there were no longer differences of gender either in Elamite or in southern Caucasian, which are neighboring languages.

The action of the substratum is manifested here in the disappearance of a grammatical category.

In spite of the richness of its nominal inflection, Letto-Lithuanian lost the distinction between masculine and neuter, even though the forms which served to express the masculine and neuter remained clearly distinct. Lithuanian final -*as* and -*a* which had to correspond to Lat. -*us* and -*um* were clear. In Letto-Lithuanian the distinction between the masculine and neuter — still existing in Old Prussian at the end of the fourteenth century — is abolished. There is a specific tendency here, and we can attribute it to mixtures of Finnish populations with those who spoke Letto-Lithuanian.

More characteristic than the losses are the innovations. In Indo-European verbal stems expressed « aspect » : durative (present), the process pure and simple (aorist), the accomplished process (perfect), the process coming to an end (determined aspect), etc. They never expressed tense. The future did not have its own expression. The distinction between the present and the past was expressed by differences of endings which also served for other usages or by the augment, which is an accessory word found in only one dialectal group : Indo-Iranian, Armenian, and Greek. Celtic and Italic have widely developed the expression of tense by verbal stems, and tense has become a dominant element in the Celtic and Italic conjugations. Celtic and Italic are not « mixed » languages for all that ; for tense is expressed by new processes which are different in Celtic and Italic, in Osco-Umbrian and Latin, and even in Oscan and Umbrian.

Nearly everywhere in Indo-European case forms cease to suffice to indicate concrete relations : to designate the place where one is, the place where one is going, one adds prepositions to the cases, until the prepositions are a complete substitute for case forms. Not only has Lithuanian maintained a strongly characterized locative which is sufficient, but it has formed an illative distinct from the accusative. It is true that the locative and illative take postpositions ; but from the Lithuanian point of view, the forms of these cases have the character of pure and simple case forms. Here again, the agreement with the Finnish type is striking. But not one Finnish grammatical form for all that has penetrated into Lithuanian or Latvian.

To understand the development of languages, it is important to note the opposition of specific tendencies to general formulas. Innovations and preservations thus assume a significant value which they would not have otherwise.

It goes without saying that it is not sufficient to recognize specific innovations either to determine the « substratum » on which a newly adapted language has been developed or even to justify affirming the existence of a foreign substratum. But we thus have the means to pose the question and a first beginning to answer it.

Whatever we may think of « substratum », it is necessary in every case to distinguish changes which characterize a language from normal changes. When we consider extended periods of evolution, some characteristic innovations nearly always stand out.

X.

NEED OF NEW INFORMATION

The conclusions hitherto enumerated are of different types. Some concern historical facts : Italian, Spanish, Portuguese, French, and Rumanian are divergent forms taken by Latin. Others express general possibilities : a consonant placed between vowels is subject to alterations which an initial consonant or a post-consonantal consonant escapes. But the procedure of proof is the same in both cases. We can say : the agreements among Italian, Spanish, etc. are such that they exclude chance ; the differences of treatment between intervocalic consonants and initial or protected consonants are such that they exclude chance. The whole methodological problem thus rests on the estimation of chance : the linguist, observing that dice often fall on the same side, concludes that they are loaded. But how many agreements and what agreements must one encounter in order to consider as excluded the fortuitous character of encountering them ?

One cannot seek to apply the calculus of probability. For the agreements are not of the same sort or of the same value. The calculus of probability is usefully applied only to facts qualitatively identical and having a common measure. Such is not the case with linguistic facts.

From the very fact that the quality and the particular details should be evaluated in each case, it depends on the tact, the judgment, and the good sense of linguists to take from the facts that part which is appropriate. All linguists do not sense things in the same way. One who may have a correct idea of phonological changes may understand poorly the way in which speakers behave in relation to a given word ; the talents and the knowledge which allow one to understand well the development of grammatical forms are not those by means of which the capricious acts of « folk etymology » are guessed. This « personal coefficient » explains many differences among linguists. And there are mistaken persons who are not capable of estimating the correct value of any comparison. But with practice and an examination of series of well established facts, an experience is acquired by means of which different types of compared facts can be correctly judged. Here are some examples of delicate comparisons where one will perceive the difficulties of proof.

It is established that intervocalic consonants are treated differently from initial consonants both in Brittonic and in Goidelic. What tends to indicate that there is a common tendency there is the fact that the intervocalic treatment is applied in both groups to the initial consonants of words closely connected with preceding words in the sentence. But the result is different in each group : in Goidelic intervocalic voiceless stops become voiced spirants : t goes to p and k to x ; in Brittonic, on the other hand, these stops become voiced : t goes to d and k to g. The change is not applied to voiced geminates which are more strongly articulated than the simple stops. The difference of treatment between the Goidelic and Brittonic voiceless stops must be due to properties of the two languages considered ; for in Goidelic certain consonants voiced by nature tend to become voiceless, but this does not happen in Brittonic. In Goidelic initial w has become f, whereas in Brittonic it has become gw ; in Goidelic initial y has become h which has been lost, whereas y remained in Brittonic. The linguist observes the coincidence. Whoever admits that the form of phonological changes is due above all to the phonological structure of the language will consider the coincidence as significant. But perhaps not everyone will subscribe to this conclusion.

The agreements of special facts have the more value the less these facts correspond to general tendencies. To establish that the Italic languages come from the same common language (of Indo-European origin) as the Celtic languages, we have several coincidences. One of the most curious is the fact that the old form of the numeral « five », which is *$penk^we$ (pañca in Sanskrit, pénte in Greek), went to Italo-Celt. *k^wen-k^we, as is seen from Irish coic and Latin quinque.

The value of the agreement is difficult to determine. It is known that the situation is not peculiar to this numeral ; the same phenomenon is found everywhere where p and k^w are found in two successive syllables in Italic and Celtic. The innovation does not apparently result from a specific tendency of Italo-Celtic. Assimilations of this type arise from general tendencies to assimilation in two successive syllables (type of *sešuras* becoming *šešuras* in Lithuanian). But what it would be necessary to know is the strength of this tendency ; but we do not know this. There are few occasions to observe the succession $p...k^w...$ It is certain that there was in western Indo-European a relationship between k^w and p and that everywhere, regularly in Greek (with definite limitations), in Osco-Umbrian, and in Celtic, sporadically in Germanic, k^w became p. The passage of $*p...\ k^w...$ to $*k^w...\ k^w...$ in Italo-Celtic is one of the facts which indicate this relationship. But the assimilation did not take place in Greek ; thus Italic and Celtic have here an innovation which opposes them to Greek. In Germanic there was an assimilation, but in the opposite direction, and in place of $*k^w...\ k^w...$ there was $*p...\ p...$ represented by *f-f* in an isolated example ; cf. Gothic *fimf*. It is seen from this that the tendency toward assimilation was natural, but that the form of assimilation had two possibilities. What characterizes Italo-Celtic is, on the one hand, the direction in which the assimilation took place and, on the other hand, the constancy of the phenomenon. The agreement is probative, but less than it seems at first sight.

Fortunately, the comparatist often has the means of finding relatively objective proofs.

The most characteristic type of problem which is posed to the comparative historian is the establishing of an etymology by comparison. To prove a comparison, it is necessary to show that certain observed agreements cannot be fortuitous. The fact that the Armenian word *erku* « two » is to be related to Greek *duo*, *duō*, Latin *duo*, etc., as has been seen on p. 18, furnishes a good example of the type of proofs which can be employed. At first sight the comparison is surprising, and we are hesitant to accept it. In reality, it is sure, and we can easily show it.

In the first place, the series of Armenian numerals from « one » to « ten » is Indo-European. The form *erku* for « two » is the only one which may not be transparent at first sight. A borrowing, which is not very probable a priori for a numeral in an old Indo-European language where the old basic vocabulary is so well preserved on the whole, is all the less acceptable as none of the known languages near to Armenian furnishes a similar form for « two », and as we consequently do not see here how Armenian could have taken *erku* from outside.

In the second place, the numerals « three » and « four », which had plural inflection in Indo-European, have in Armenian in the nominative the nominative form with final -*kʻ*, whereas, beginning with « five », which is the first of the uninflected Indo-European numerals, there is no -*k‘* : *erek‘* «three», *č‘ork‘* «four», but *hing* « five », *vec‘* « six », etc. The numeral « two » naturally had dual inflection in Indo-European. In the historical period Armenian no longer had the dual, and doubtless had not had it for a long time ; the form *erku* thus cannot be explained at a historical date. And it is remarkable that *erku* remained without plural sign when the category of the dual was abolished in Armenian. This survival in Armenian of a trace of the Indo-European dual is striking ; it calls to mind what is observed in Lat. *duo*, Gr. *duŏ*, etc.

The treatment **erk-* of initial **dw-* is strange. But it has been shown that it is found in all the cases where this same initial group figures ; two other comparisons, as good for the meaning as that of *erku* with Lat. *duo*, establish it. And the fact can be explained in Armenian (cf. p. 46).

Moreover, if *erku* were an old dissyllable and if *e* had existed here originally, the final -*u* would not have been able to maintain itself ; for in every dissyllable which Armenian has inherited, the vowel of the final syllable has been lost. The -*u* of *erku*, which corresponds so naturally to the old **-ō* attested in Hom. *duō*, OCS *dŭva*, etc., has remained only because at the time when the vowels of final syllables were lost the word was not dissyllabic.

However, the strangeness of the phonological treatment might leave doubts in certain minds. The proof is accepted as soon as concordant variations of the form of « two » in Armenian and in the other Indo-European languages are shown. As an Indo-European ō is represented by u in Armenian, the form erku rests on *duwō, preserved for example in the Homeric form duō and in OCS dŭva, as in Vedic d(u)vắ. But there was another form *duwo with final short ŏ, which is the usual form in Greek, e.g. duo. Besides erku « two » Armenian has erko-tasan « twelve » (two and ten), where the type in short ŏ is maintained. And this is not all : in the first term of compounds, Indo-European had *dwi- and not *dwo- ; cf. Sanskrit dvi-, Greek di-, Latin bi- ; Armenian has erki- in erkeam « two years old ». This triple series of concomitant variations excludes chance.

The proof is thus accomplished.

It is not always possible to find agreements so complete and so numerous. Thus the degree of probability of etymologies varies from one case to another. In some cases, as that which has just been cited, the proof leaves nothing to be desired and attains a degree of rigor which is rarely found in historical material. In others, the comparison is only possible, and sometimes it is difficult to show even its likelihood. Between the two extremes there are all degrees of probability ; one of the most serious faults of many etymological dictionaries is that they do not adequately indicate the differences of value among the comparisons. If the linguist has no coefficients to note these differences, nonetheless he does not lack the means of making them felt and of signalling them.

To make historical linguistics advance, it is important to specify, systematize, and extend research. For the theories rest on incomplete and vague data presented by chance rather than chosen.

More precise observations are always necessary : whenever data have been observed more closely, new results have been obtained. For the languages presently spoken, we are far from making use of all the means at our disposal. Phonetics requires laboratories and linguists trained to handle the instruments in these laboratories. And it is not enough to observe facts as they are at a given moment. A recent article of the late Poirot, which appeared in the *Mélanges Andler*, has shown how a change can be perceived and its mechanism can be seen at the very moment when it is realized. For the ancient languages, the linguist must have recourse to a philology of precision : it has sometimes been imagined that the linguist can be content with philological approximations ; he needs, completely to the contrary, all that the most exact philological methods permit him of precision and rigor.

It is necessary to institute systematic research. Almost nothing has been done hitherto to establish linguistic theories by methodical research. Some psychologists alone have begun series of experiments the majority of which have not been followed up by others.

It would be important, for example, to study with care to what degree acquired linguistic habits are transmitted from generation to generation. It is not known whether a child learns the language of its parents more easily than it could learn a different language, and especially a language of a different type. There is a complete investigation to be made here, and one which does not present particular difficulties.

Certain facts would lead us to believe that the children of parents who know several languages well or the children of bilingual parents would be more apt to learn different languages well themselves than the children of parents both of whom speak only one language.

The fact that similar innovations seem to appear about the same time among children born under the same conditions would result from the inheritance of acquired habits.

Here one catches a glimpse of a whole set of observations and even of experimental research which might throw a new light on linguistic development.

Moreover, the experience of linguists is too narrow. If the great languages have often been described in minute detail, the local dialects are far from being described with enough precision. Apart from the great languages, we have only few exact descriptions ; it is necessary to see how languages of types as different as possible function, and under conditions as varied as possible.

A more serious thing is the fact that there is hardly any state of language which has been observed and described in an exact, precise, and complete way. What phonological descriptions, grammars, and dictionaries give are either typical cases, more or less arbitrarily chosen, or norms. But there is scarcely any domain of which we could actually say what the whole state of language is. What interests the linguist is not the norms but the way in which the language is used.

Nothing differs more from one state of language than another state of language. The dialect of a rural village where everybody is approximately at the same social level, where everybody has approximately the same culture is one thing, the dialect of a city where there are people of different conditions, of different educations, and of different cultures is another thing. A city where everybody uses the same language is one thing, a city like Istanbul where peoples speaking five or six different languages live side by side is another thing. The conditions vary with customs : in cities of the Levant, where the men know four or five languages more or less and use these languages outside according to circumstances, the women confined to the house may have only one language. The variety of situations according to the people is infinite.

We think that we know what French is. In reality no one really knows how all persons speak either in a French village or in a French provincial city, or even less in Paris. Whoever wished to know how French will evolve would have to investigate to what degree local dialects are used in the country and in the cities, what special form French assumes in each

province and in each city and, in each city, among
the people of each social position, each profession,
and each group.

The French of the grammars and dictionaries is
known ; but it is only a set of rules. What is important for the linguist is to know how the people who
speak French behave in relation to the rules. We have
only vague ideas about this ; no methodical investigation has been made, scarcely any partial probings.

And yet the fact that Common French is becoming
the language of everybody in France whereas, at the
beginning of the nineteenth century, it was the language of a very small minority of cultivated people
has radically changed the conditions of development
of the language and cannot fail to cause considerable
innovations.

What is true for French is true for all the great
languages of the world.

History establishes that common languages spread.
But insofar as the past is concerned, the way in which
this expansion has taken place is not determinable.
And as for the present which we might observe, we
let it slip away almost without notice. Before 1914
Russian became the common language in Tiflis. But
it has never been shown by what processes and by
what intermediaries. The need of having a common
language in a city where there lived side by side
people whose mother language was Georgian, Armenian, Turkish, Russian, and many other languages led
to the use of Russian, for which school and govern-

ment worked and which had the prestige of bringing civilization. But the following minor custom was able to contribute largely to it : Armenian women did not work as servants, and the well-to-do Armenian families had Russian women in their service, particularly to care for their children ; Russian thus became a mother language for a number of little Armenians, above all in the most respected and most influential families.

Berber, the old language of the country, and Arabic, the language of the invaders who brought Islamism, coexist in the colonial territories of North Africa administered by France. Arabic, which is the language of the religion and a great literary language, is tending, at least in Algeria, to eliminate Berber, which is only a set of local dialects. However, the Islamic peoples, faithful to their religion and to their traditions, are accepting from European civilization only certain of its material elements ; thus they are not adopting French apart from certain external needs. The advances of civilization which a European government is bringing are consequently leading to the abandonment of Berber and to the generalization of Arabic ; so that the French domination is working to extend the domain of Arabic without consciously wishing to do so.

In cases of bilingualism it would be necessary to know how each language acts on the other and what reactions result therefrom.

America furnishes some noteworthy examples which

it would be necessary to study in detail, and which linguists have hardly touched.

North America was colonized in the seventeenth and eighteenth centuries by colonists who were primarily English. The present country of the United States ceased being an English colony only at the end of the eighteenth century, and Canada is today a dominion of the British Empire ; some Englishmen have emigrated each year to the United States in the course of the nineteenth and twentieth centuries. The literary language has never ceased to be the same on both sides of the Atlantic ; the grammatical norms are the same ; the schools give the same grammatical instruction ; there is even an English purism among the most cultured people especially in the eastern part of the United States. On the other hand, the influence of the Indians does not exist. Some have been eliminated, others have been relocated in special regions ; there has been no mixture of whites with the old inhabitants of the country. And yet only one hundred and fifty years after the Declaration of Independence, the English spoken in America differs markedly from that which is used in England. A distinguished literary critic, Mencken, goes so far as to speak — a little tendentiously — of two distinct languages.

The divergence can be explained.

In the first place, English is less resistant to change than French. The grammar is less rigid ; English is especially characterized by idiomatic expressions which are more subject to change than are grammatical forms proper. Purism is, moreover, less strong, less organized, and less popular in England than in France.

The United States has become a strong nation which does not feel any dependence on the old country, and to which a dependence, even limited to language, would be a burden. If some intellectual groups remain tied to the old English culture, especially in the area of old colonization, the East, it is the situation with educated persons whose influence on the whole of the country is not dominant. The school system does not depend on the central government and cannot play the strong unifying role which it plays in France, for example.

And, above all, the United States is a country of immigration. Emigrants from all parts of Europe have gone there : Irish for whom, even if they spoke English, English was the result of a not very old acquisition, Germans, Scandinavians, Latvians and Lithuanians, Poles, Russians, Finns, Rumanians, Jews from Eastern Europe, Italians, Greeks, Armenians, and even Syrians. English is the common language of the United States ; but this common language is spoken by many persons whose mother language was different or who, even if they were born in the United States, have heard a different language from their parents. In the majority of areas, these new emigrants are much more numerous than the descendants of the old colonists. English is thus spoken in the United States by a majority of people for whom the tradition of English is recent, and of whom many are still bilingual. As the importance of the central and western parts of the United States grows, where the proportion of recent immigrants is greater than in the East and where there are fewer British traditions, the language runs a greater risk of being corrupted.

In sum, there are few conservative forces but many forces which tend toward change. The fact that English is already evolving in a different way in the United States than in England is only natural.

It would be singularly instructive to follow the destiny of English in the world.

In its intention to examine a complex domain such as that of the languages of the Caucasus, the Institute for the Comparative Study of Civilizations thus has a correct idea of the most urgent needs of linguistics. Investigations of this sort will furnish precise and complete information on states of languages and will thereby permit doctrines to be changed. We await with confidence the results which such an investigation will give by means of the labors of fine, trained observers and of very experienced linguists, and it is hoped that these results may soon evoke similar investigations in other domains. On these investigations and on the rigor with which they will be conducted depends the future of linguistics.

ACHEVE D'IMPRIMER
LE 10 MARS 1967
PAR EXPRESS-IMPRIMERIE
8, RUE VICQ-D'AZIR
PARIS (10ᵉ)